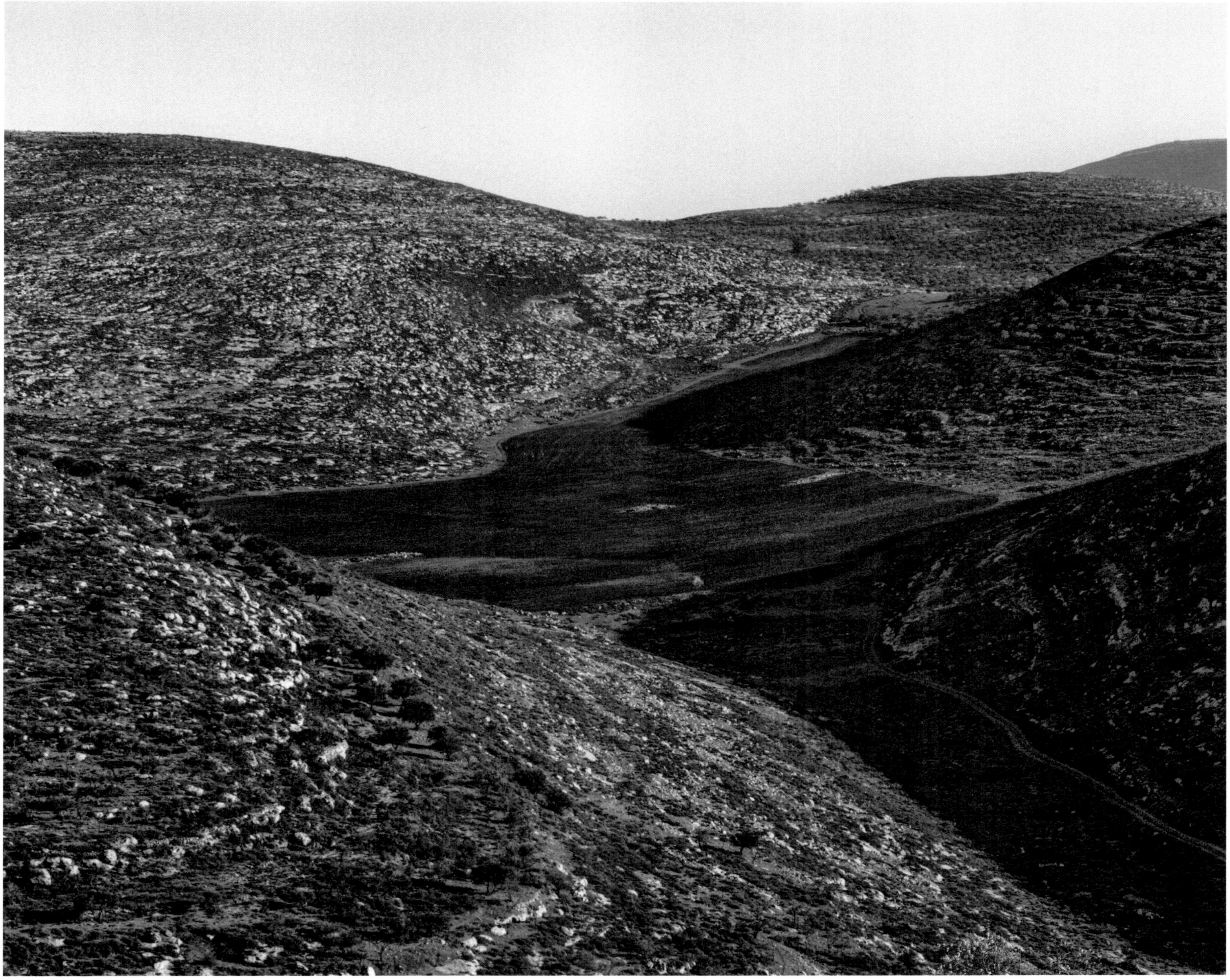

GOST

Ken Taranto

THE SETTLEMENTS

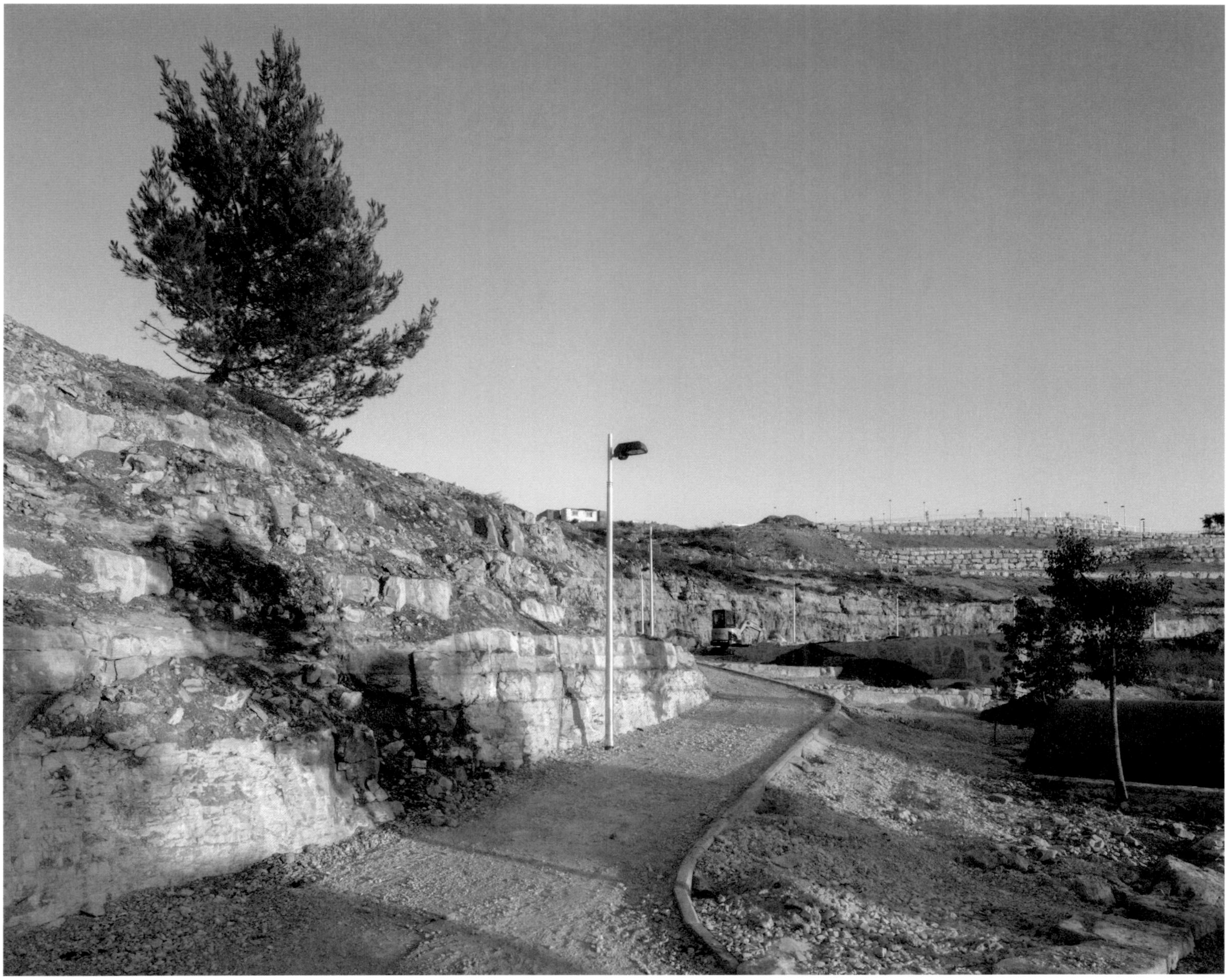

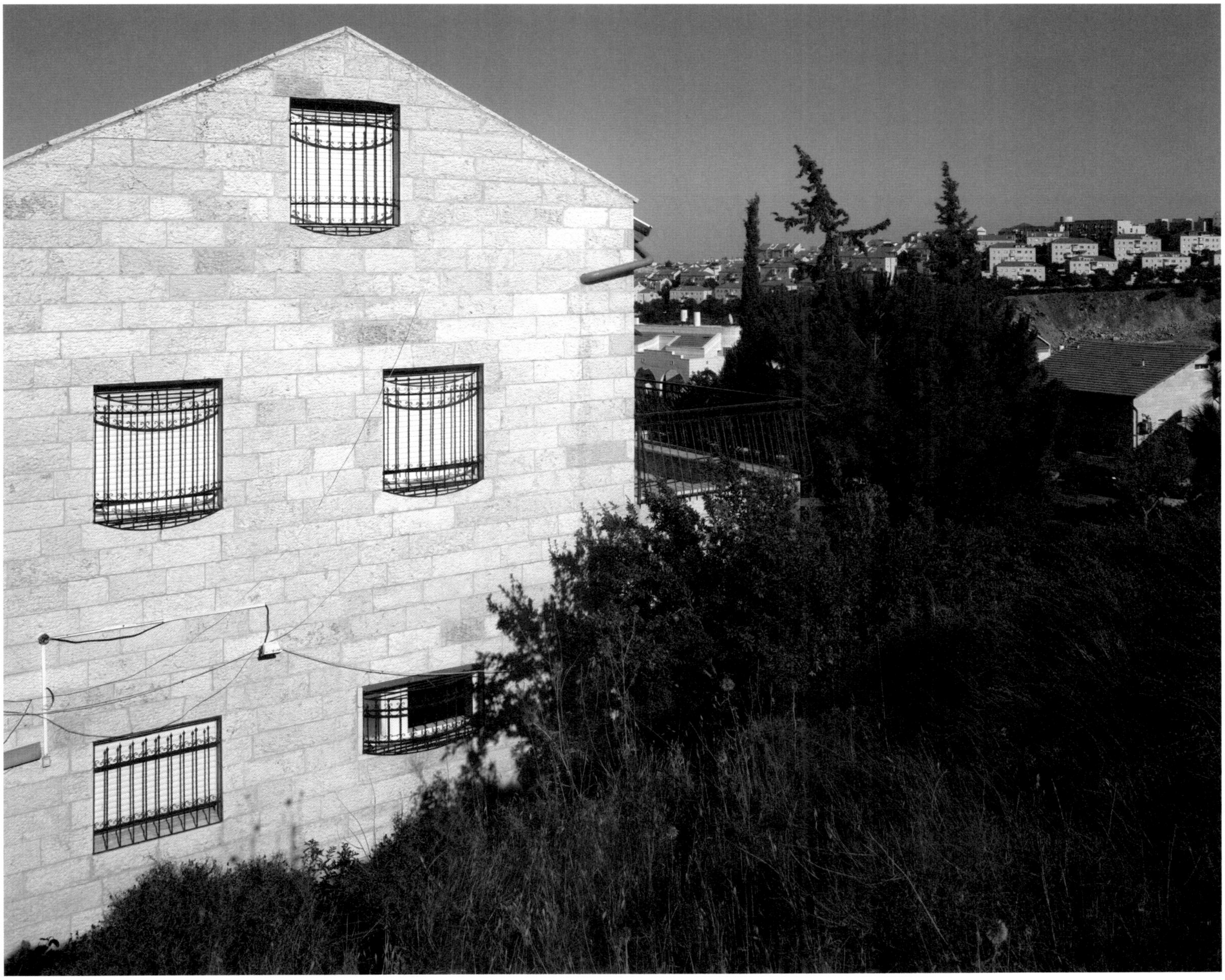

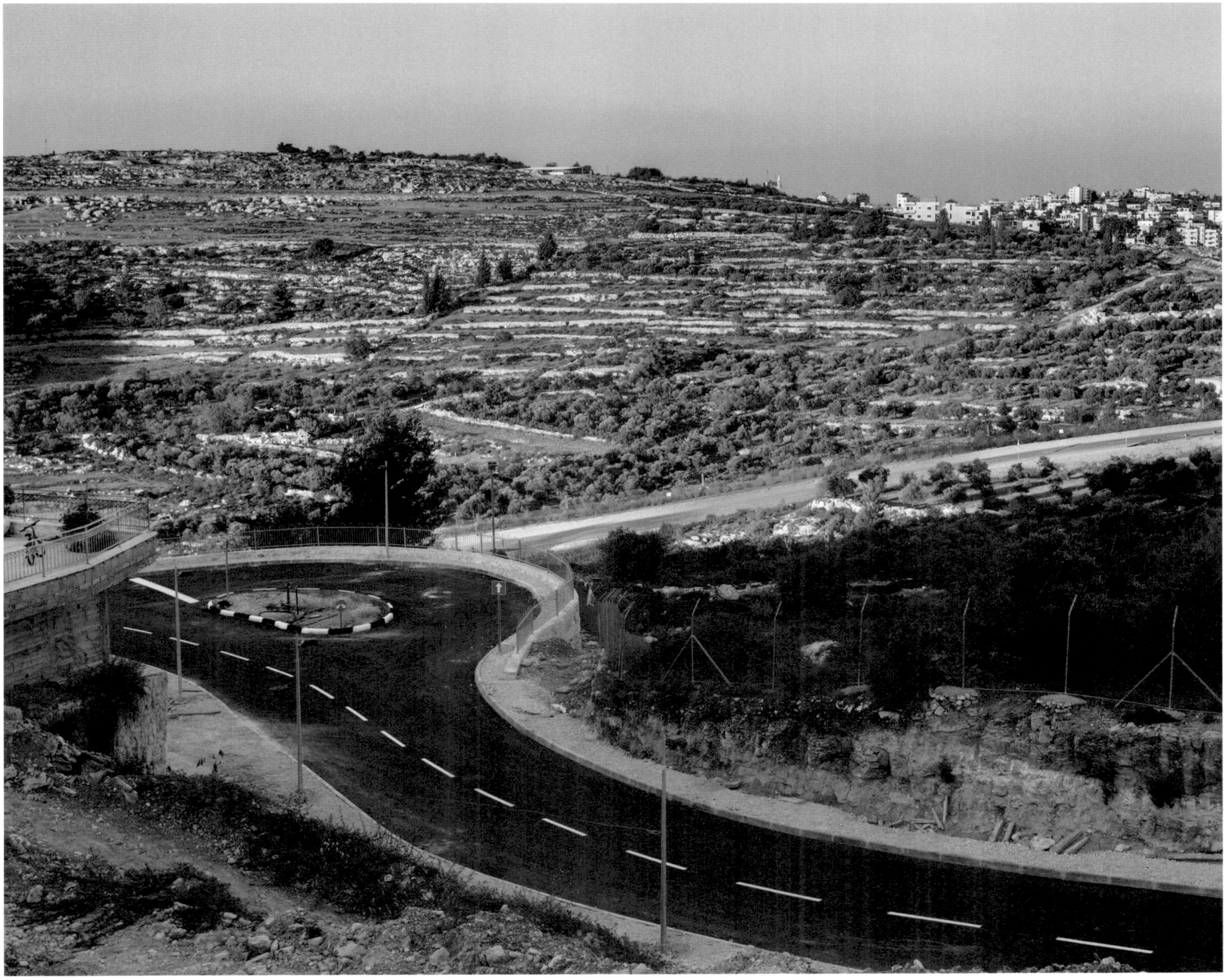

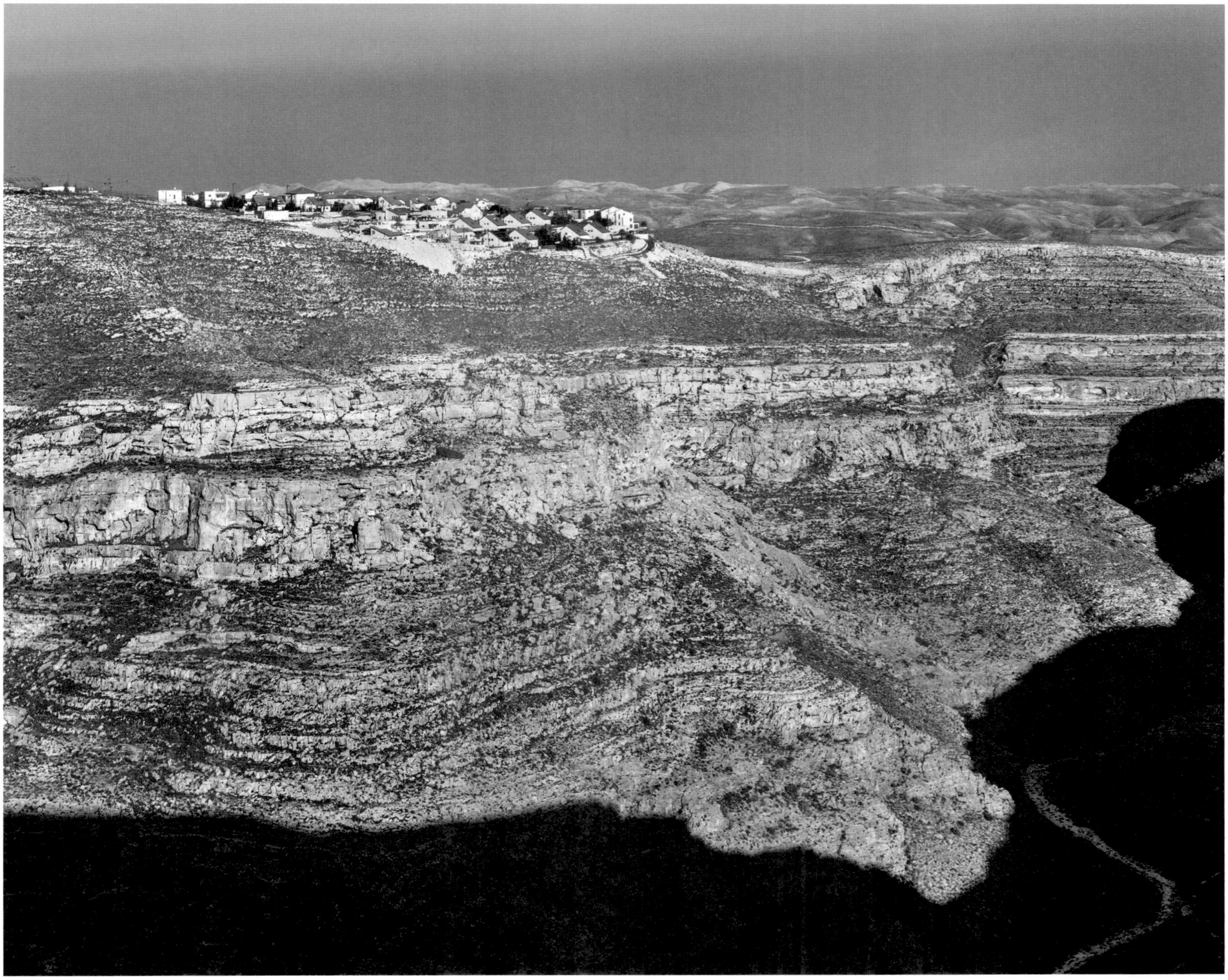

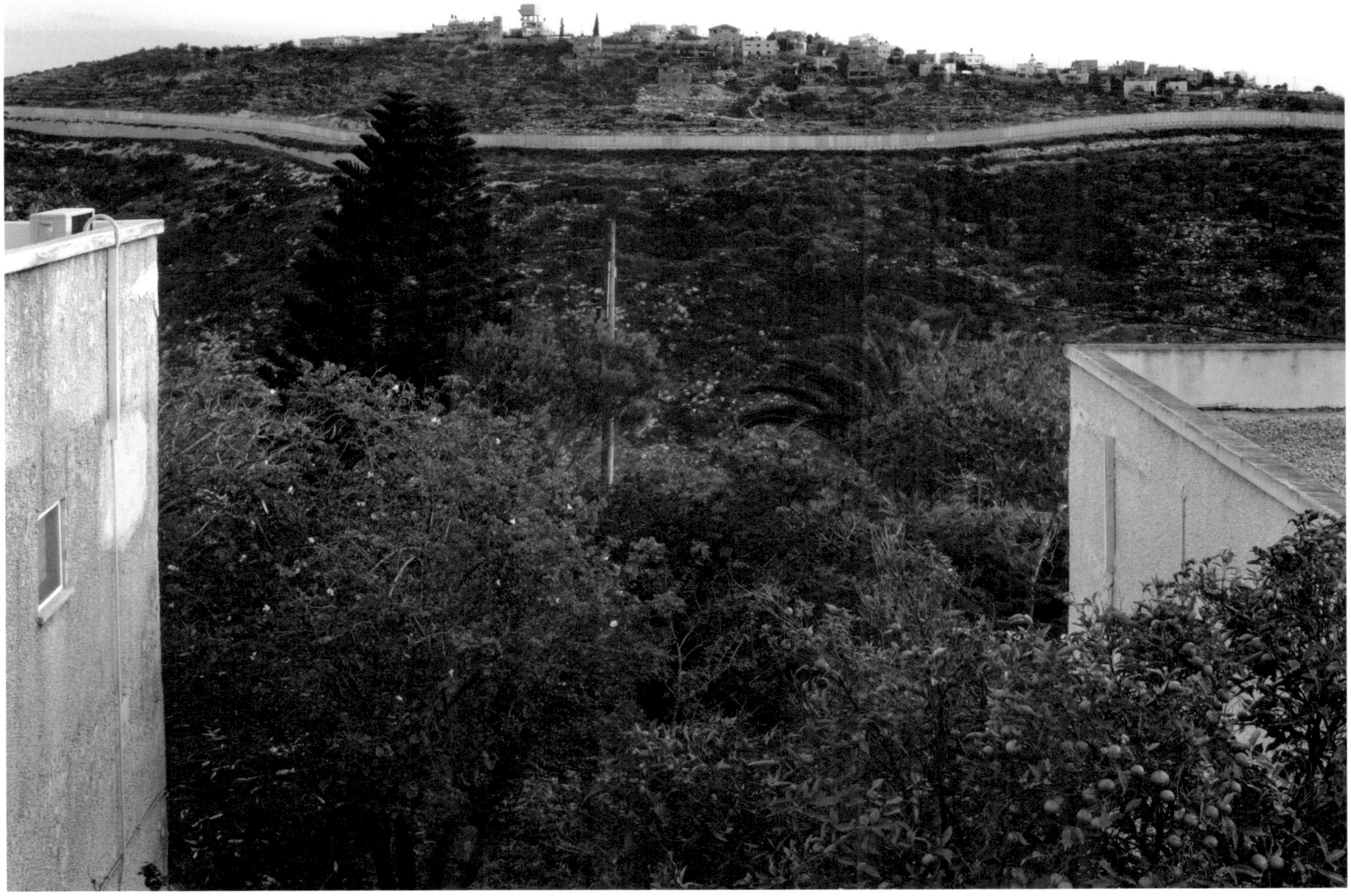

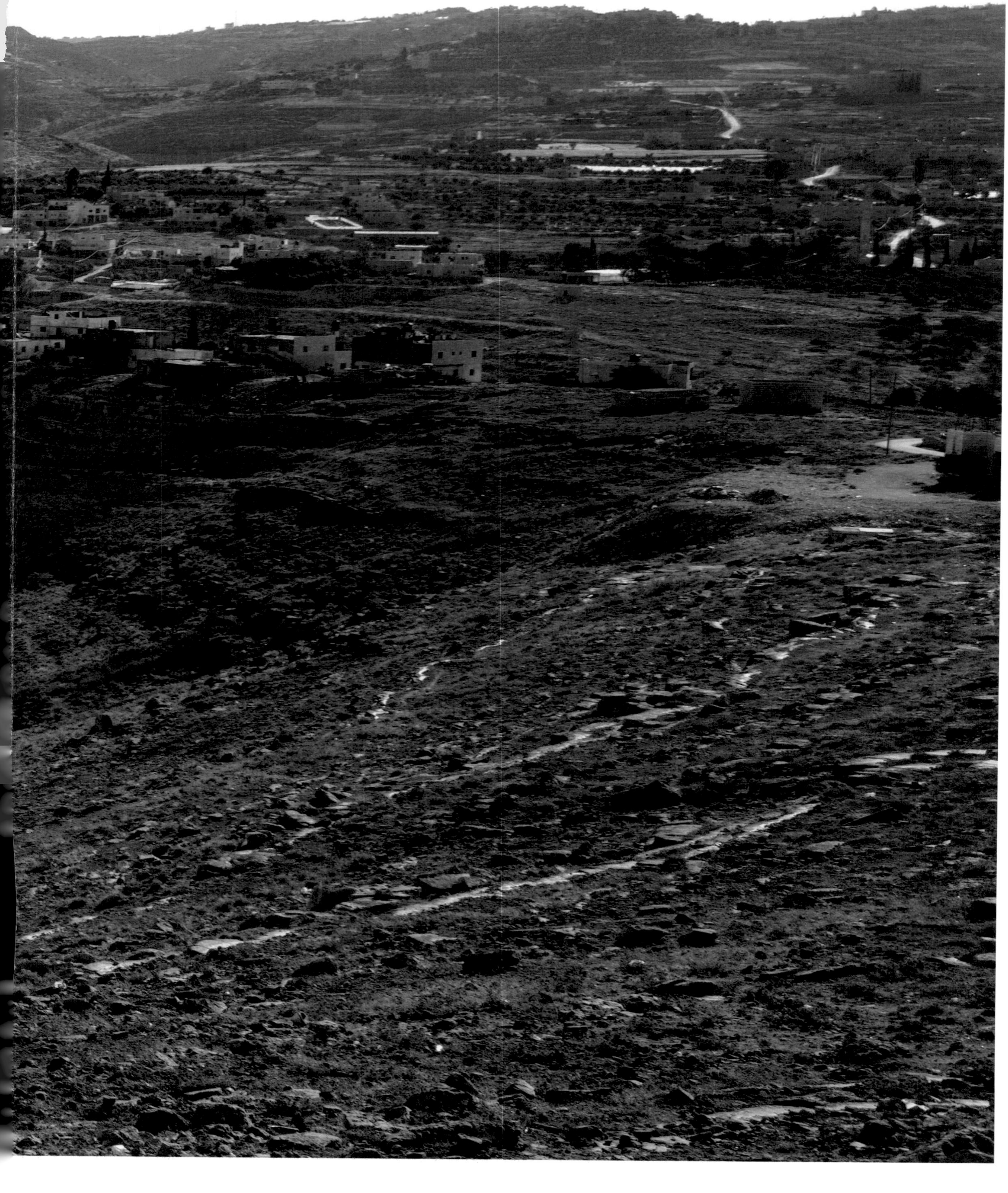

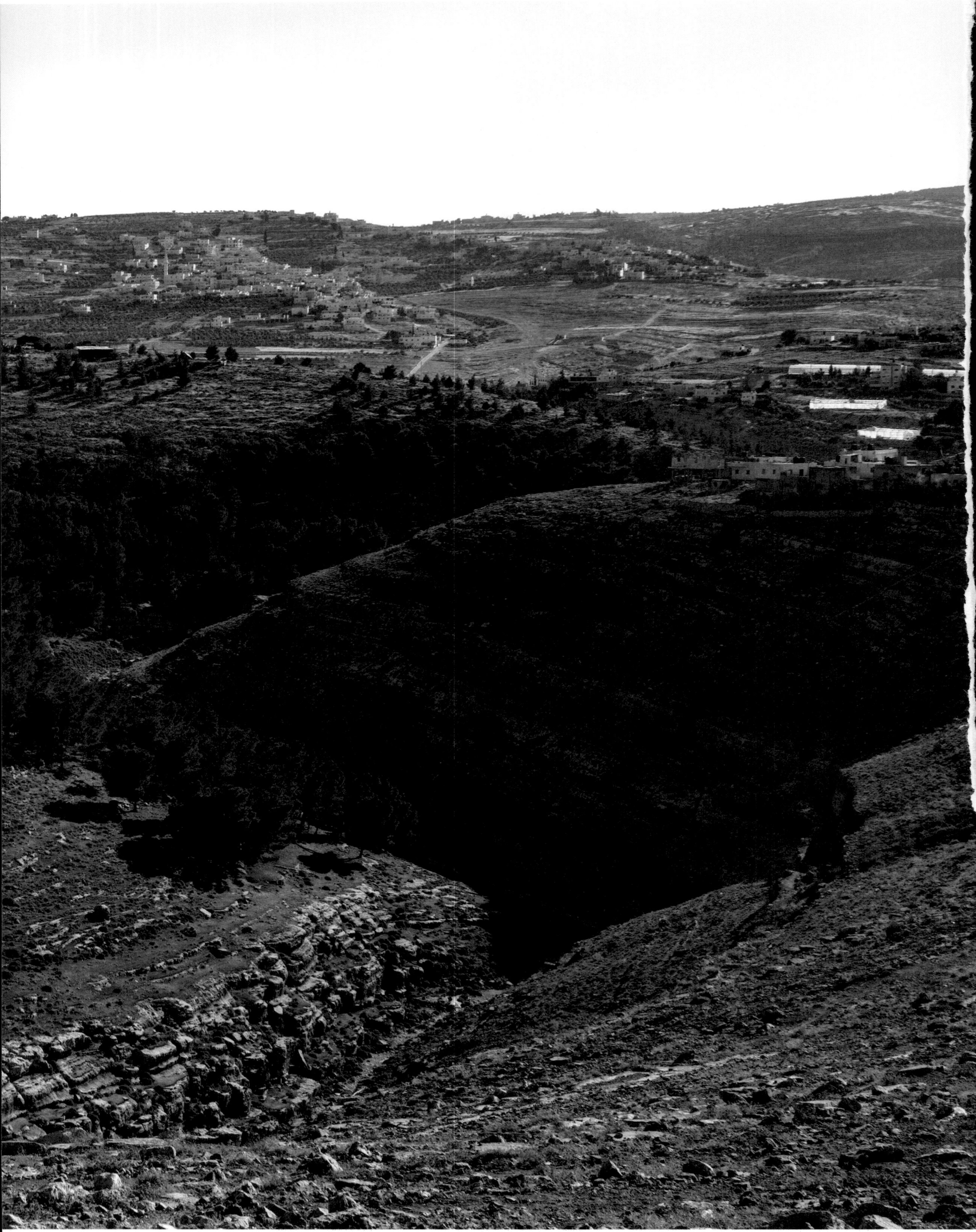

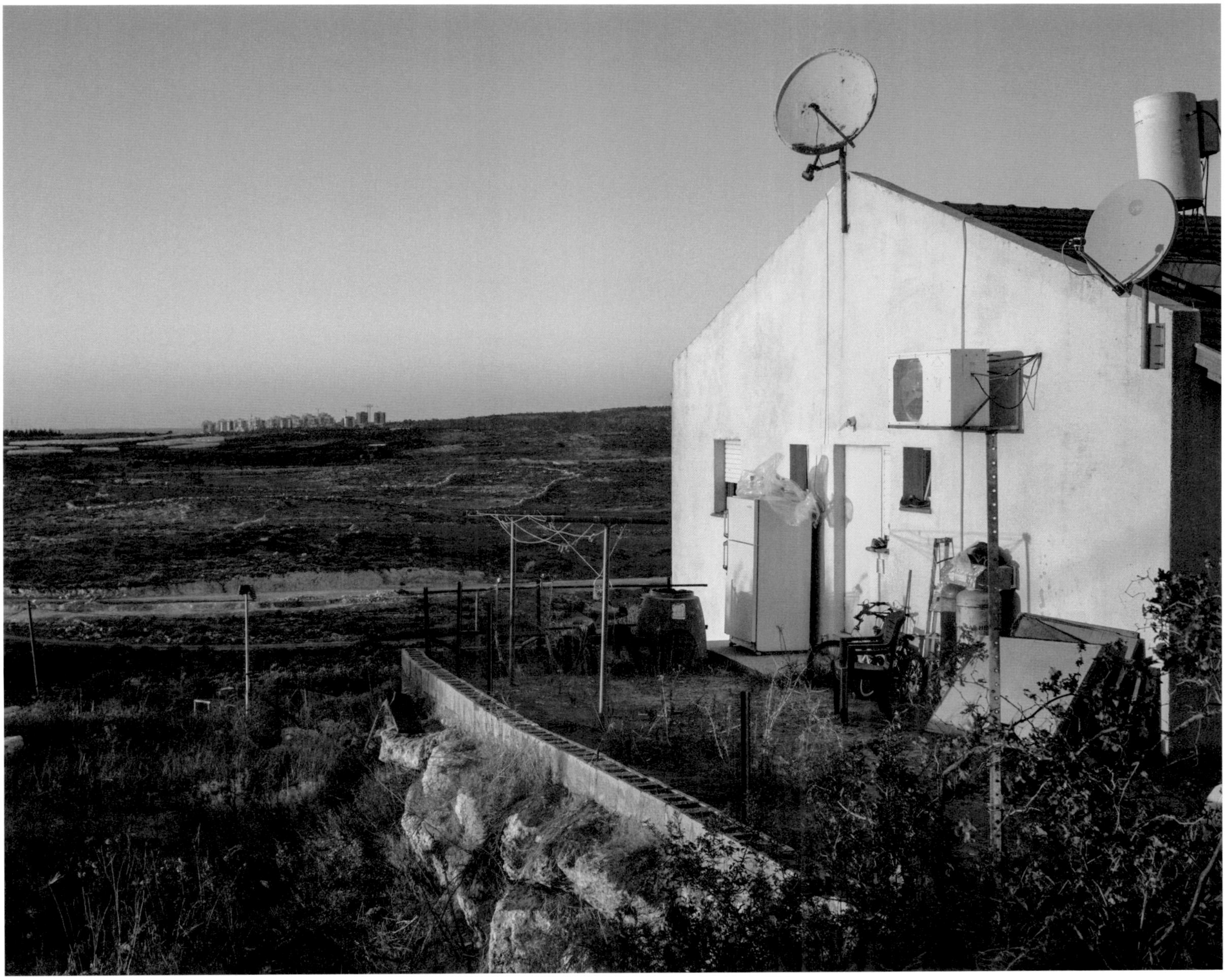

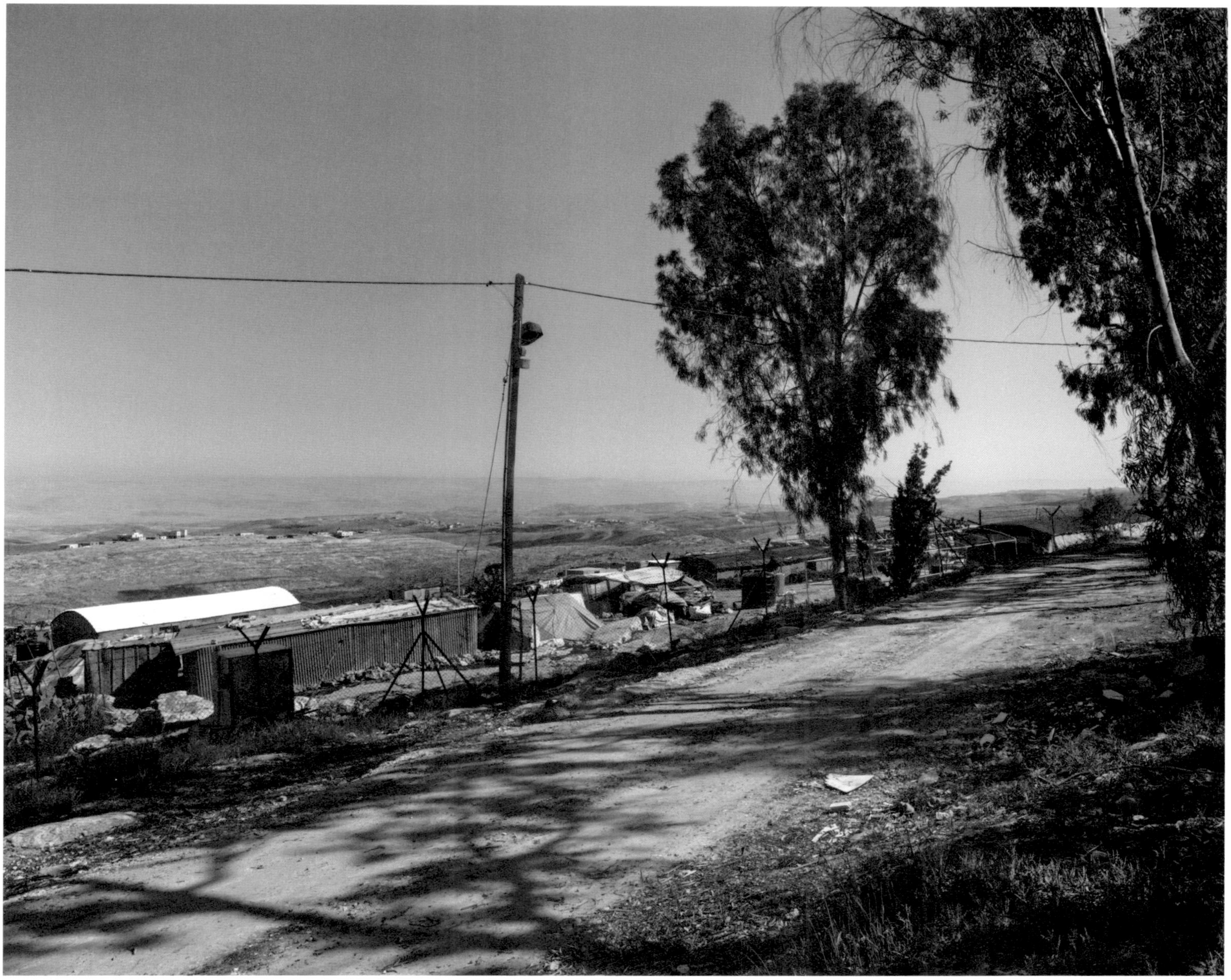

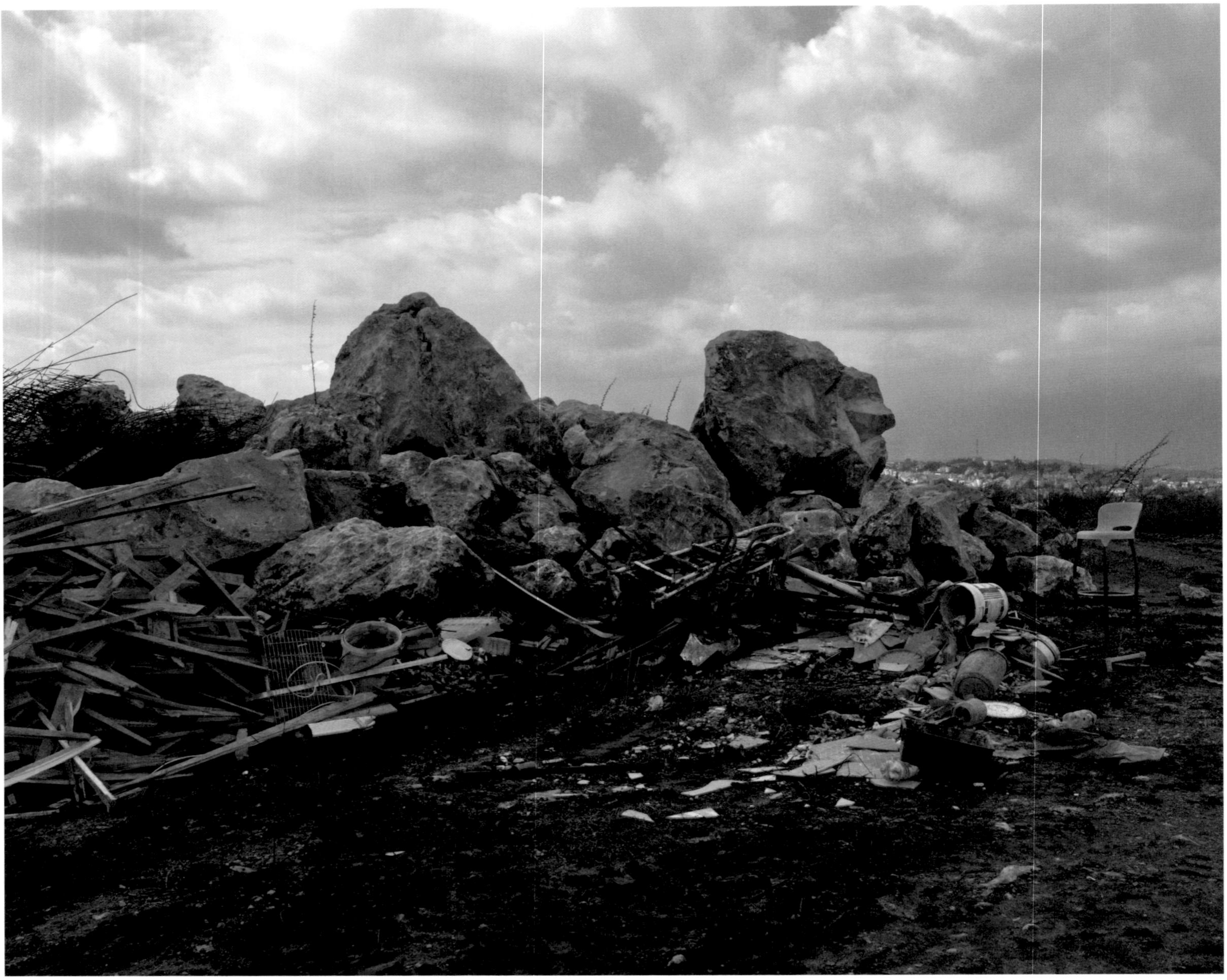

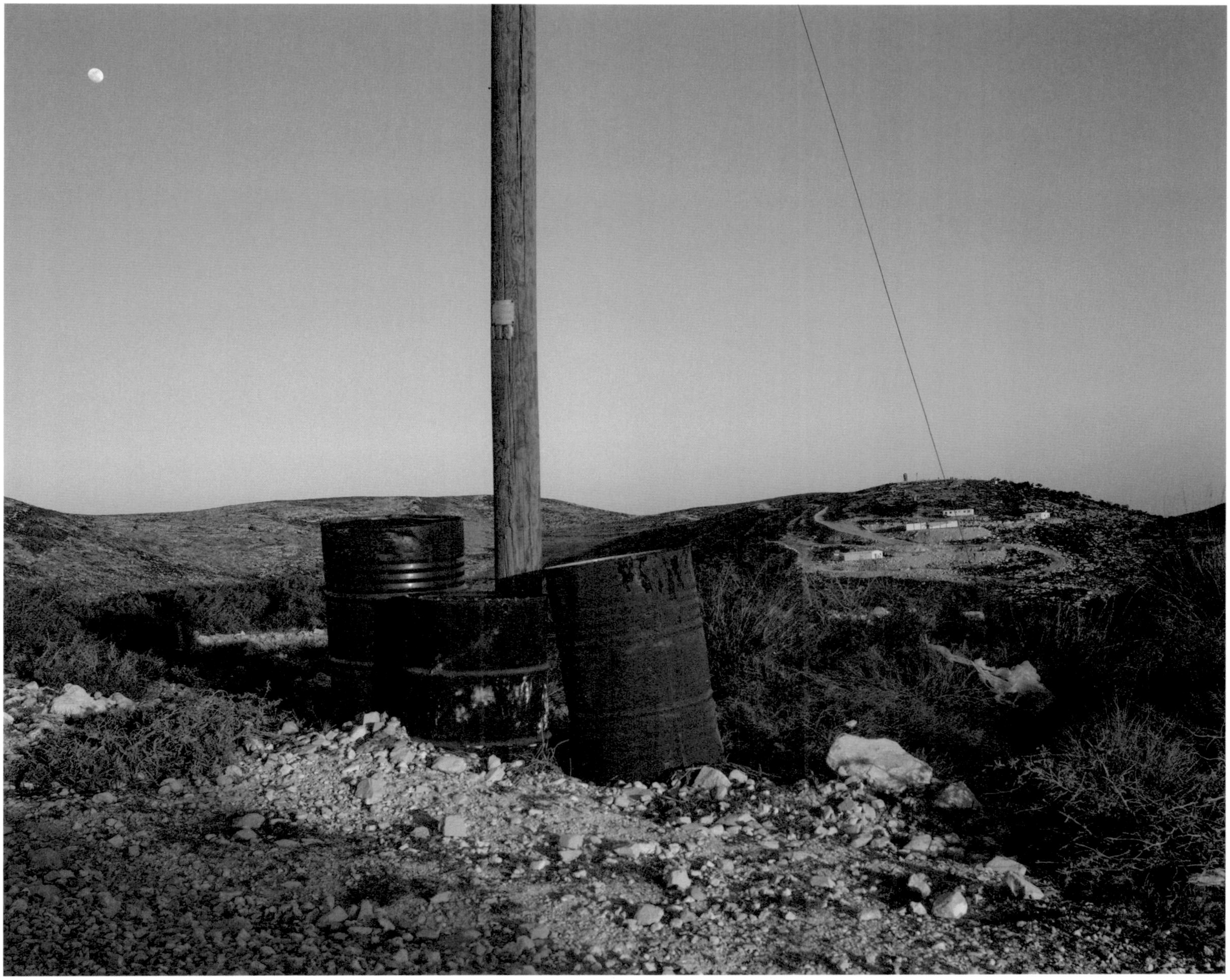

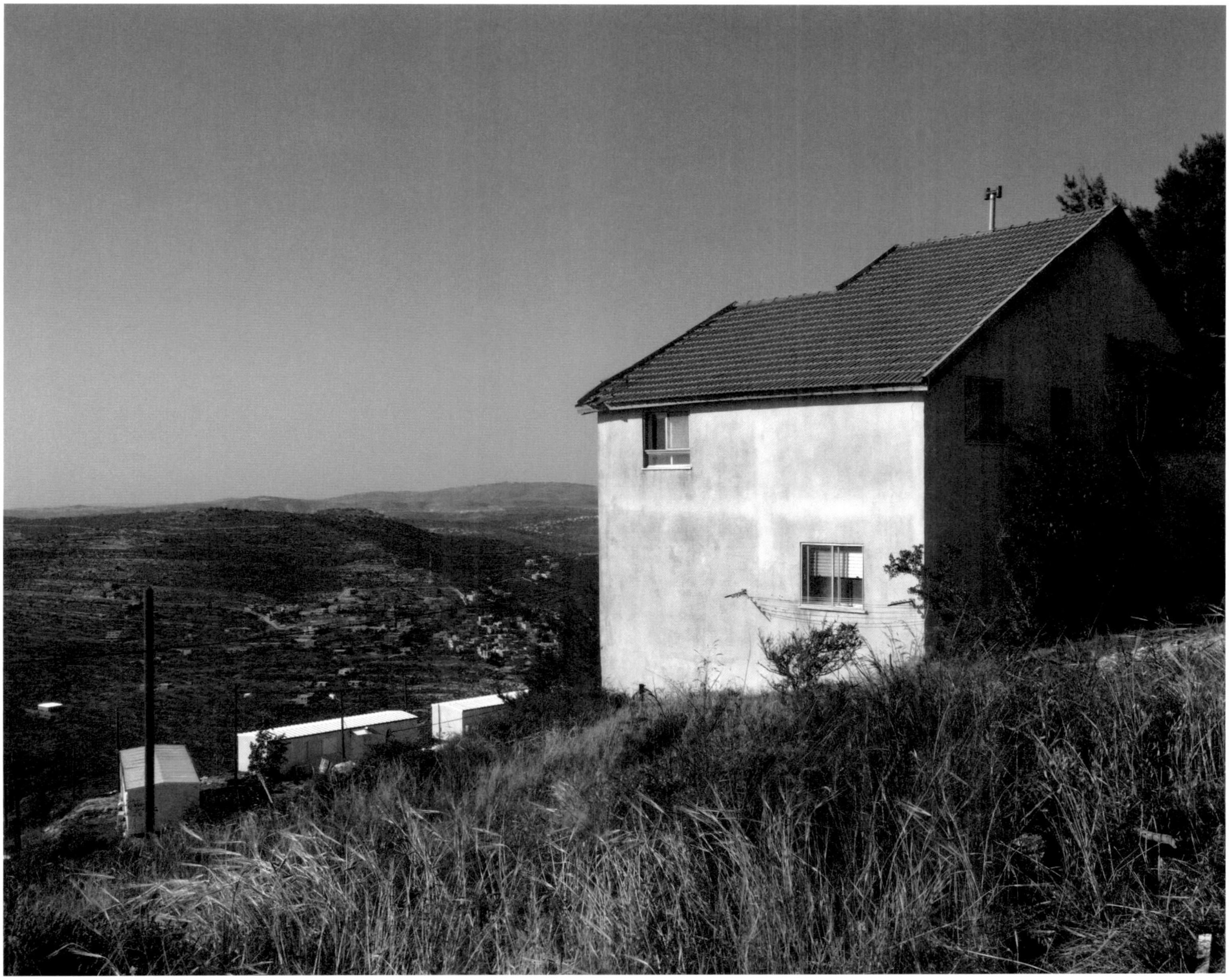

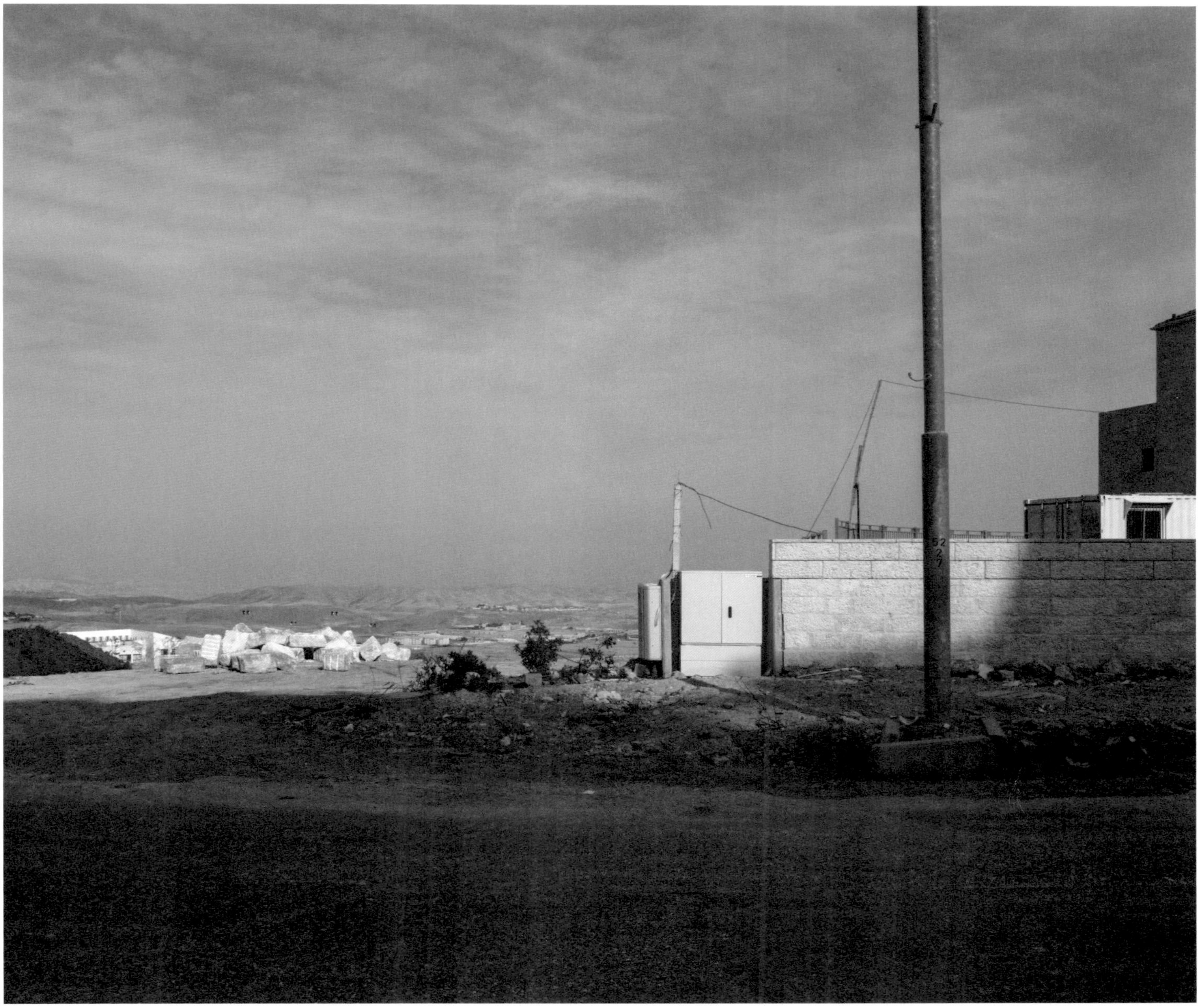

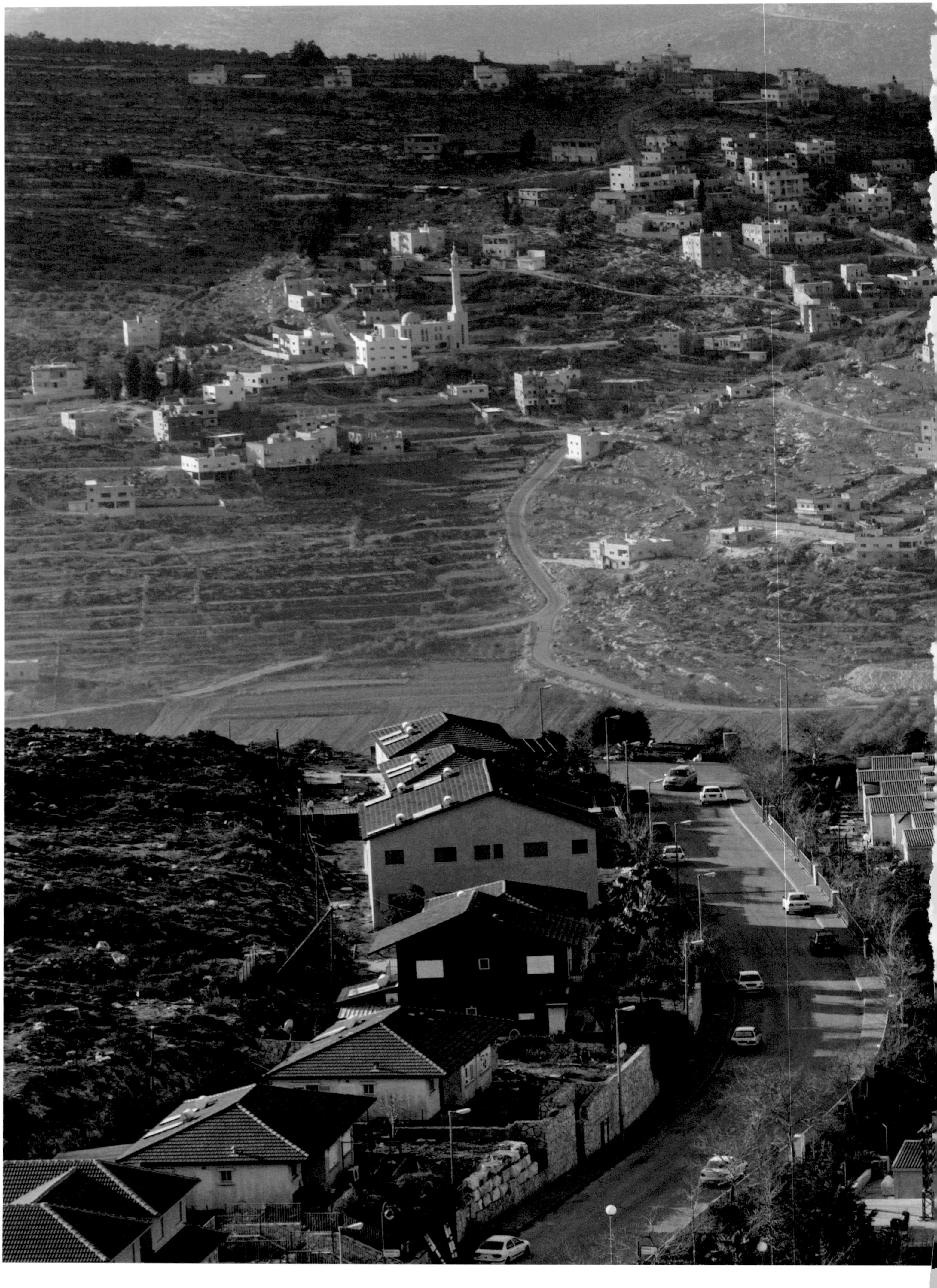

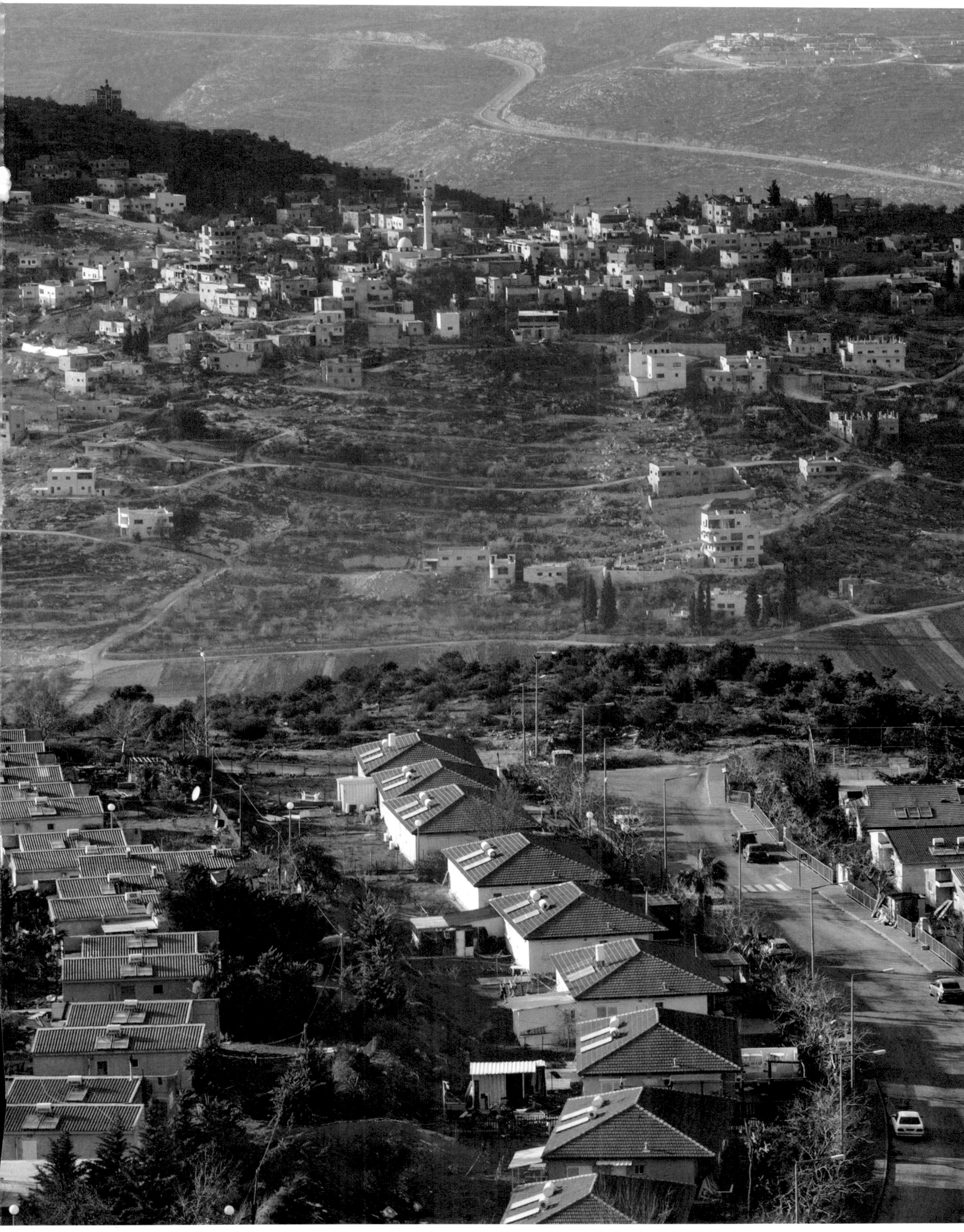

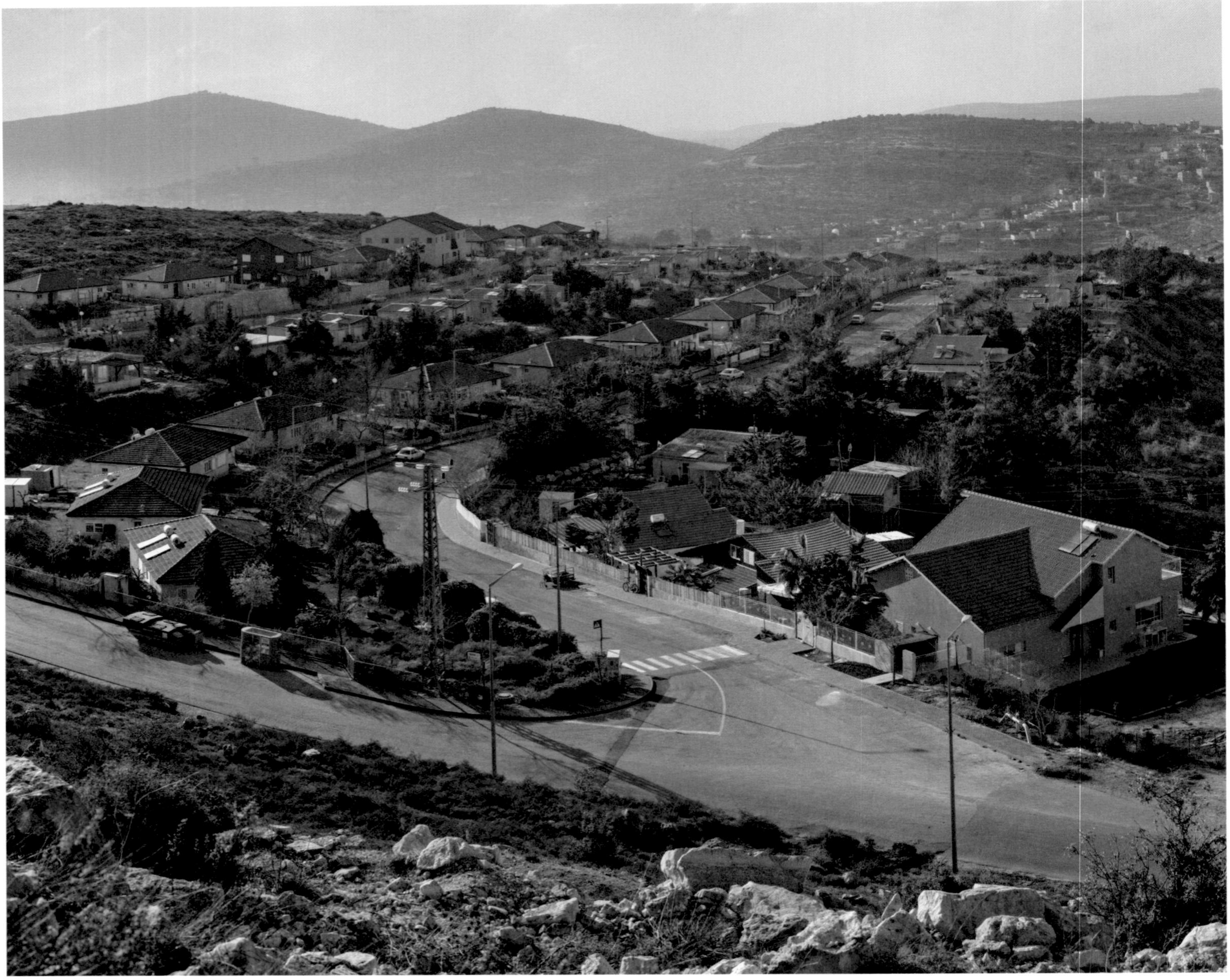

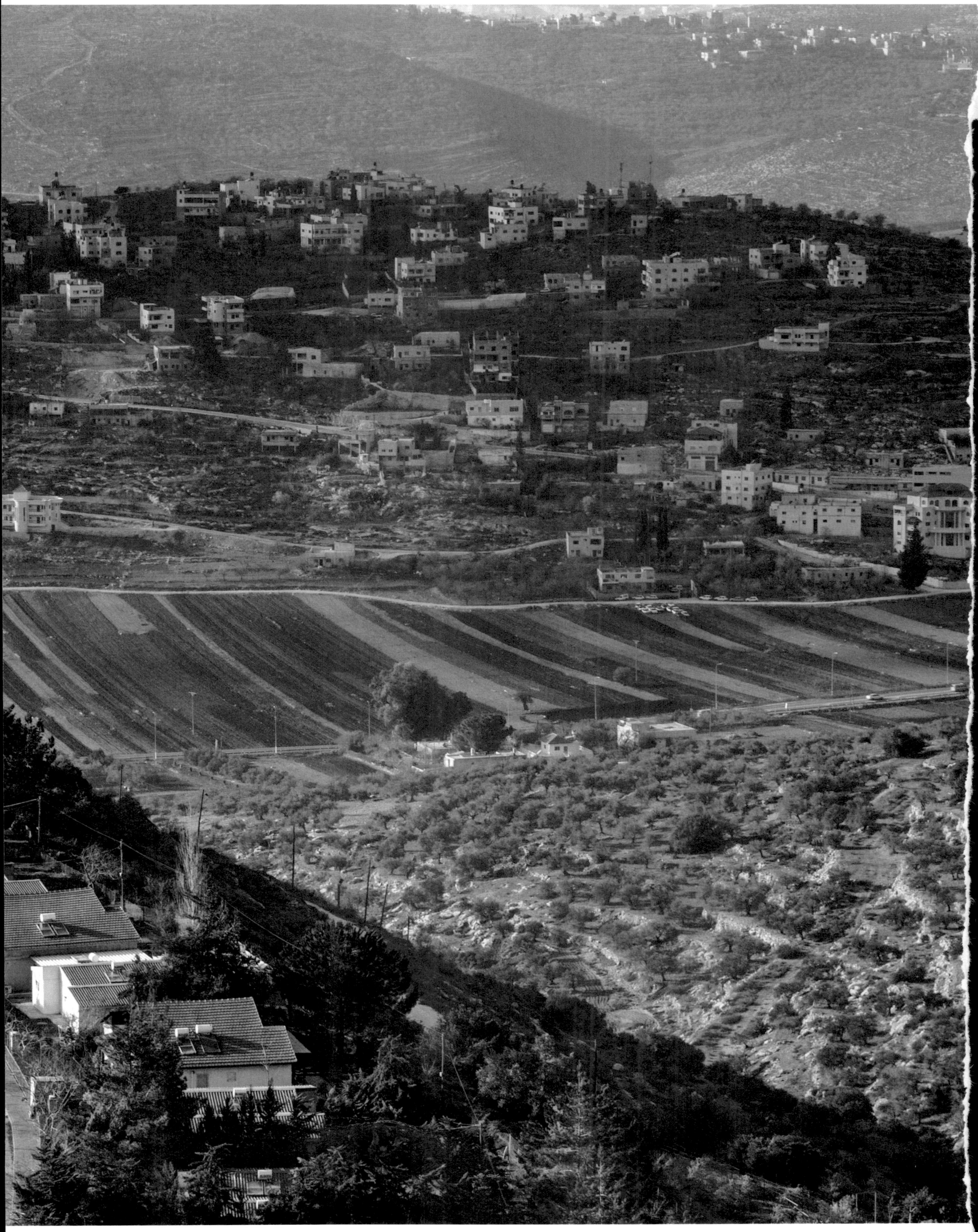

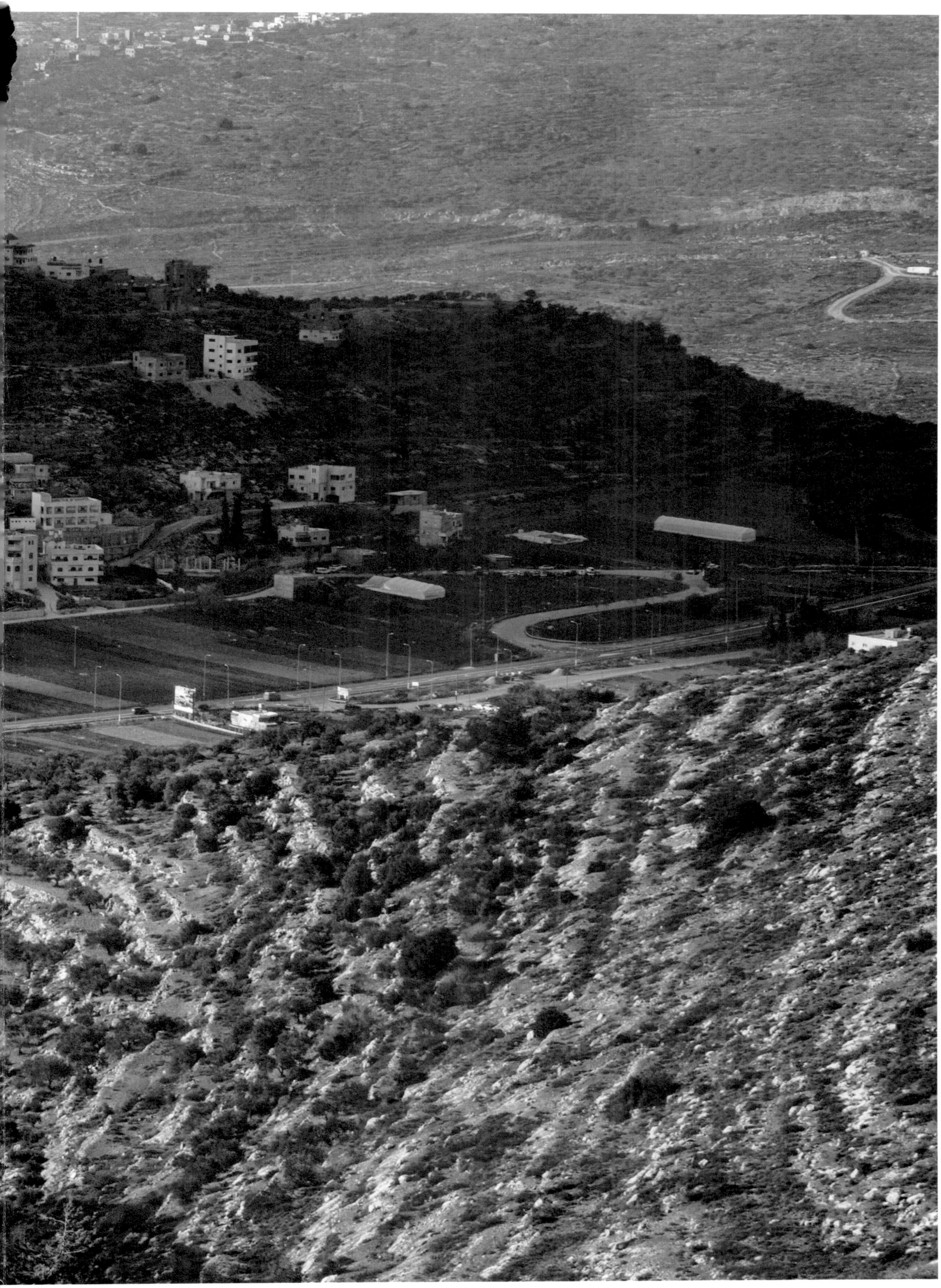

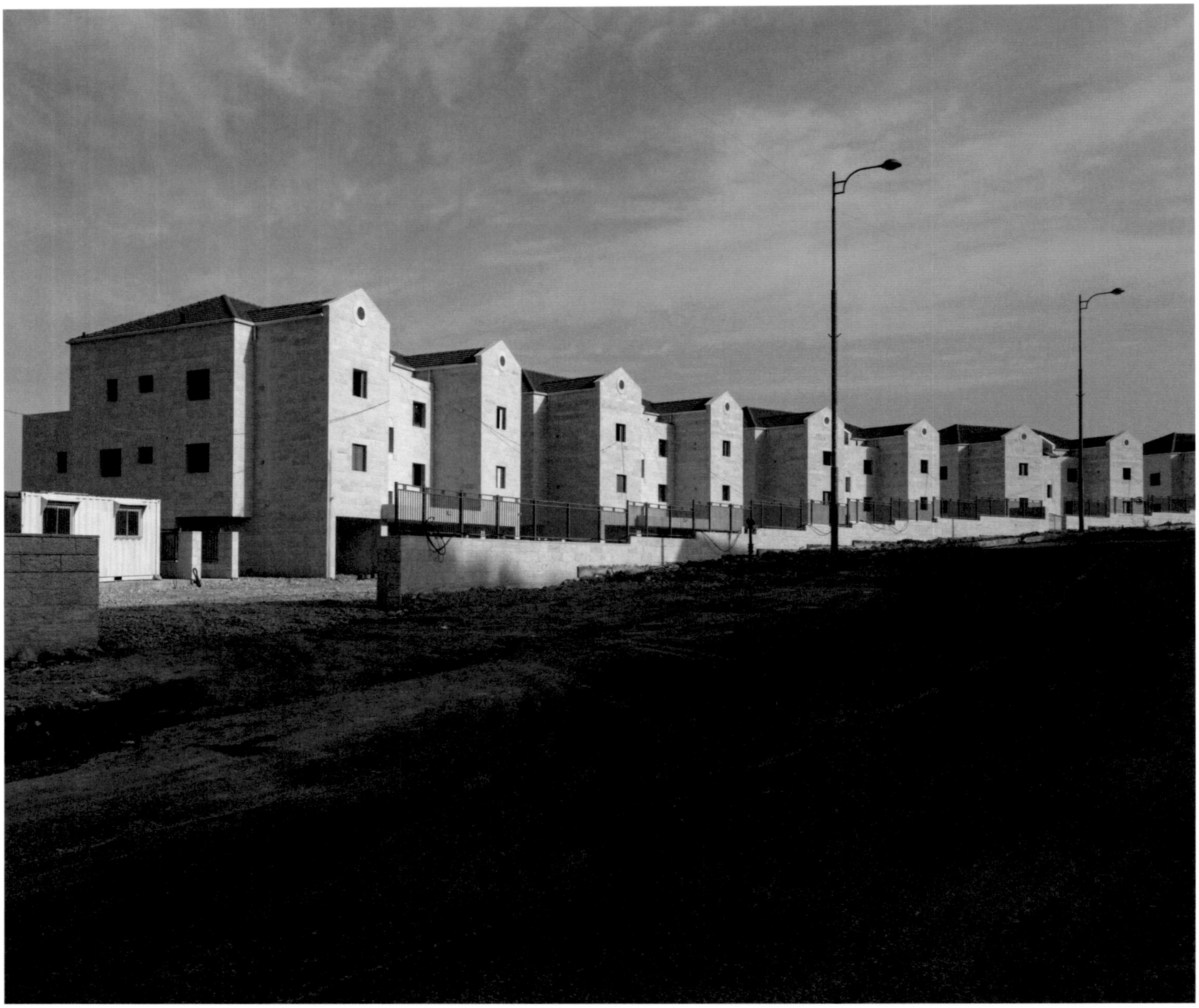

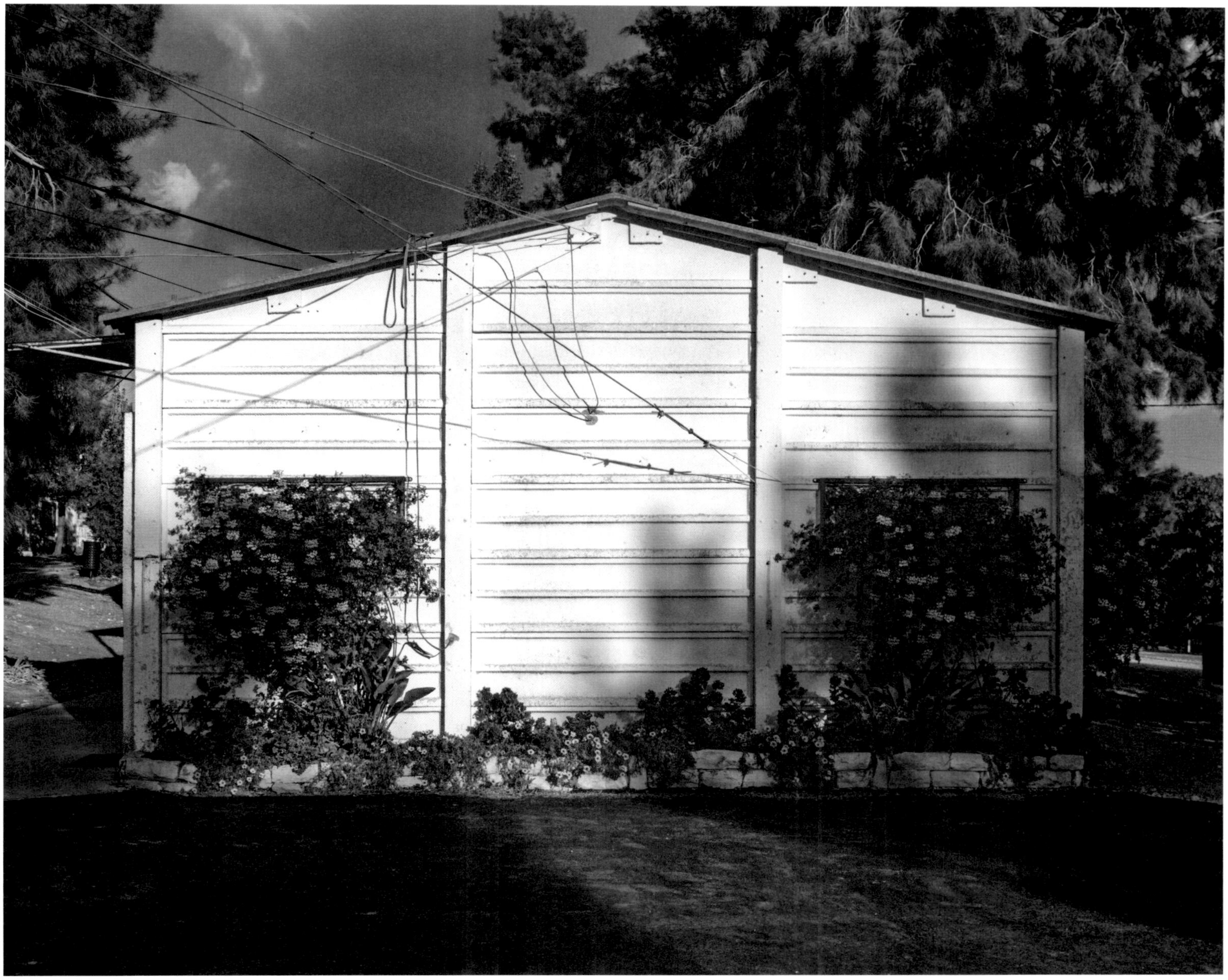

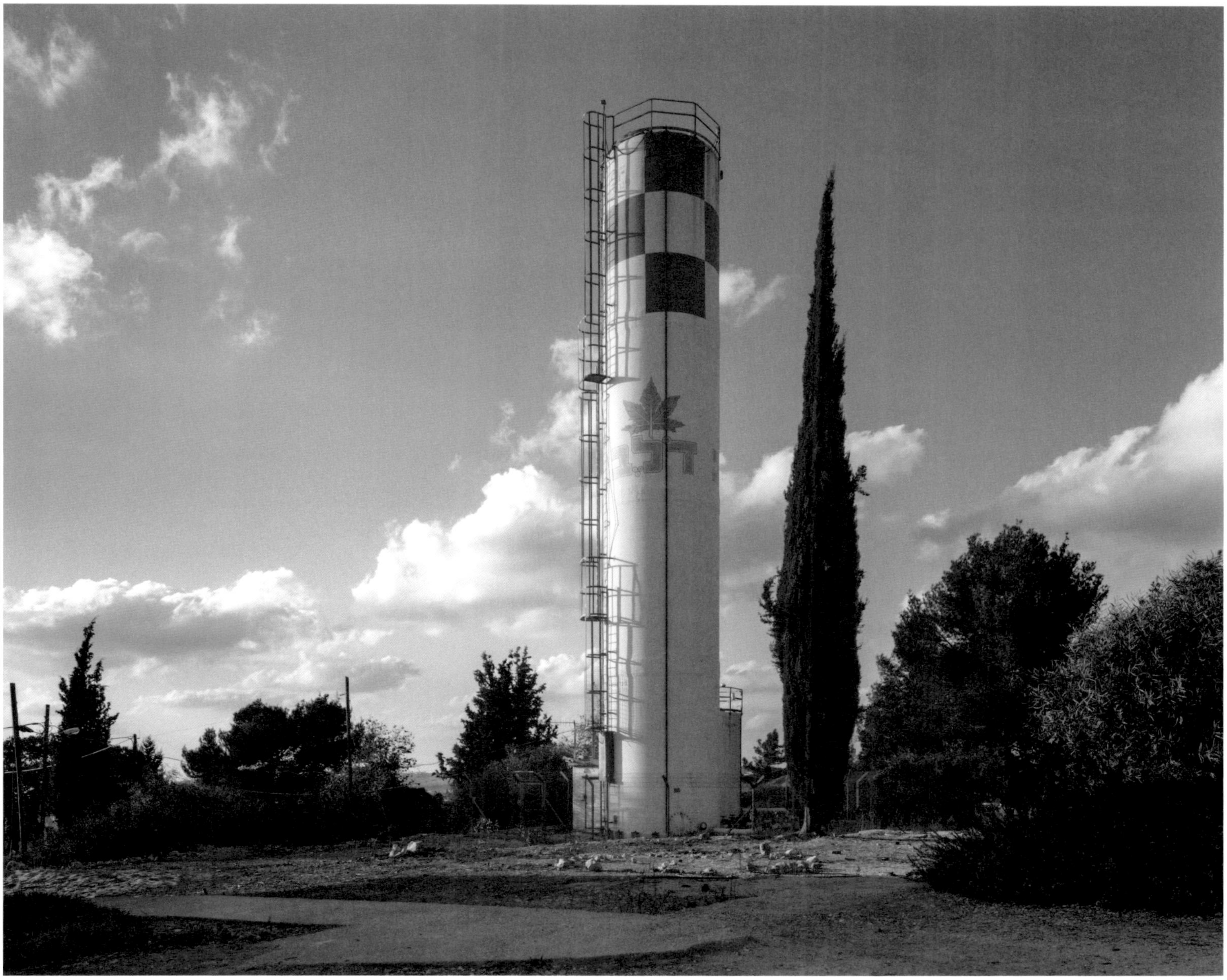

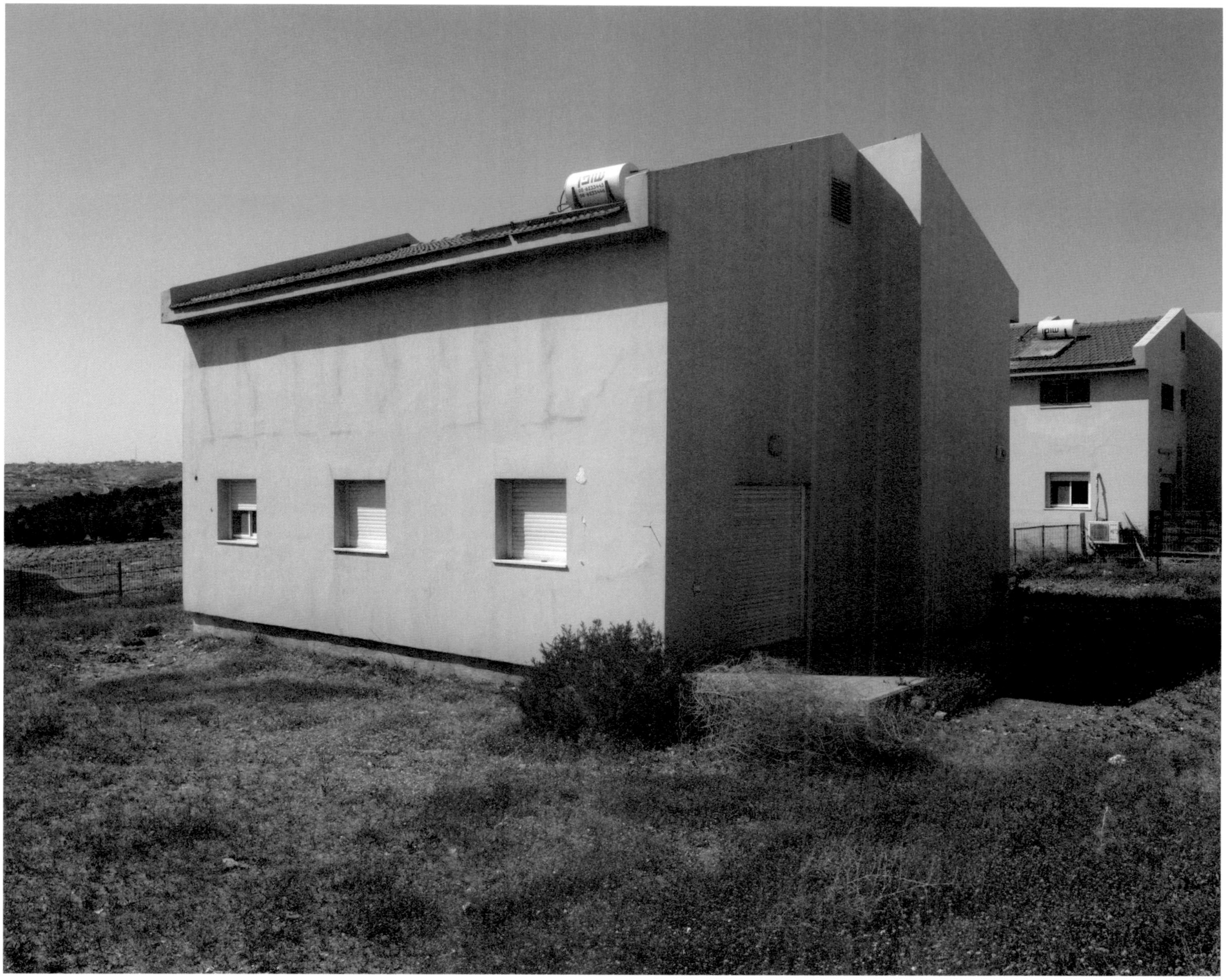

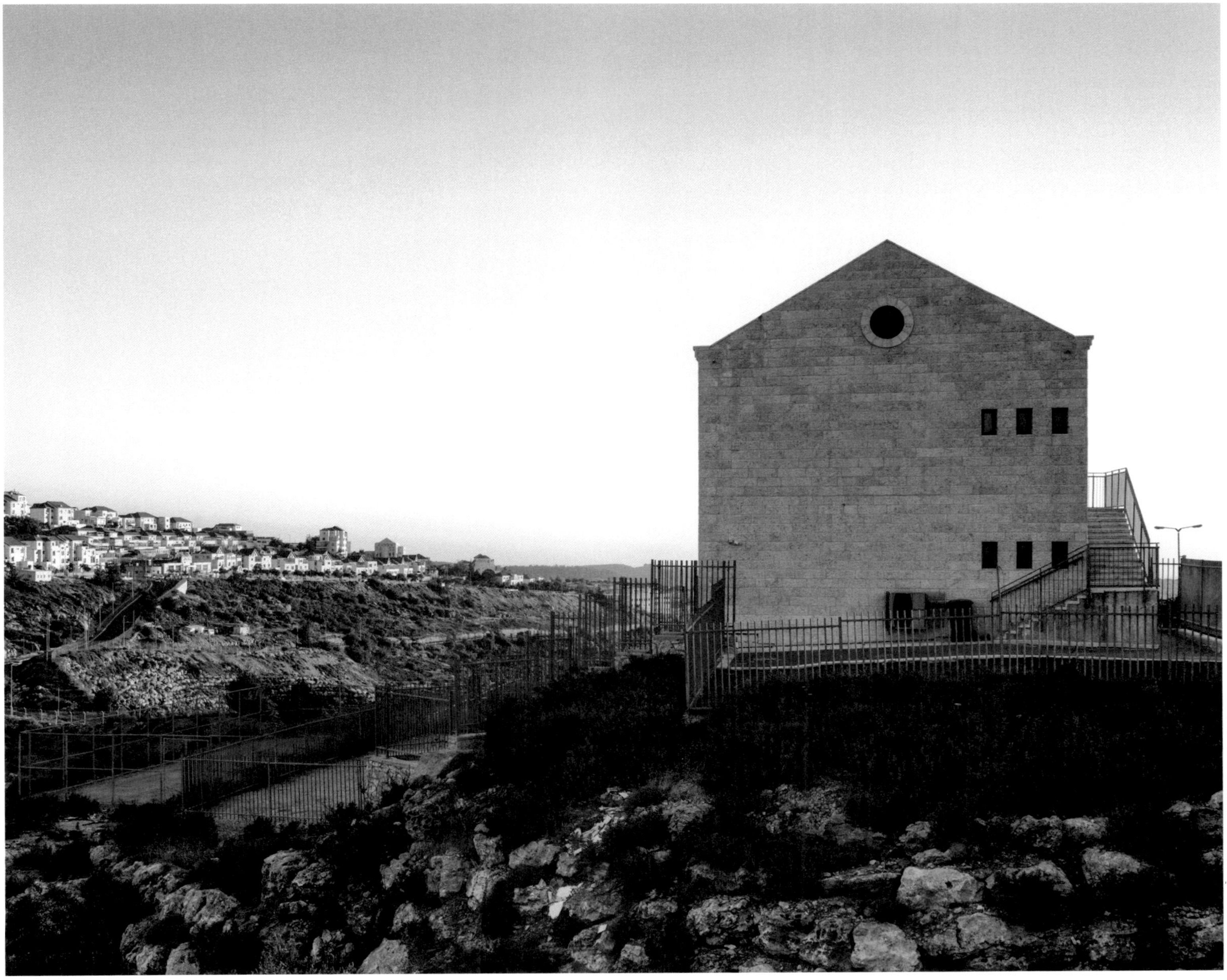

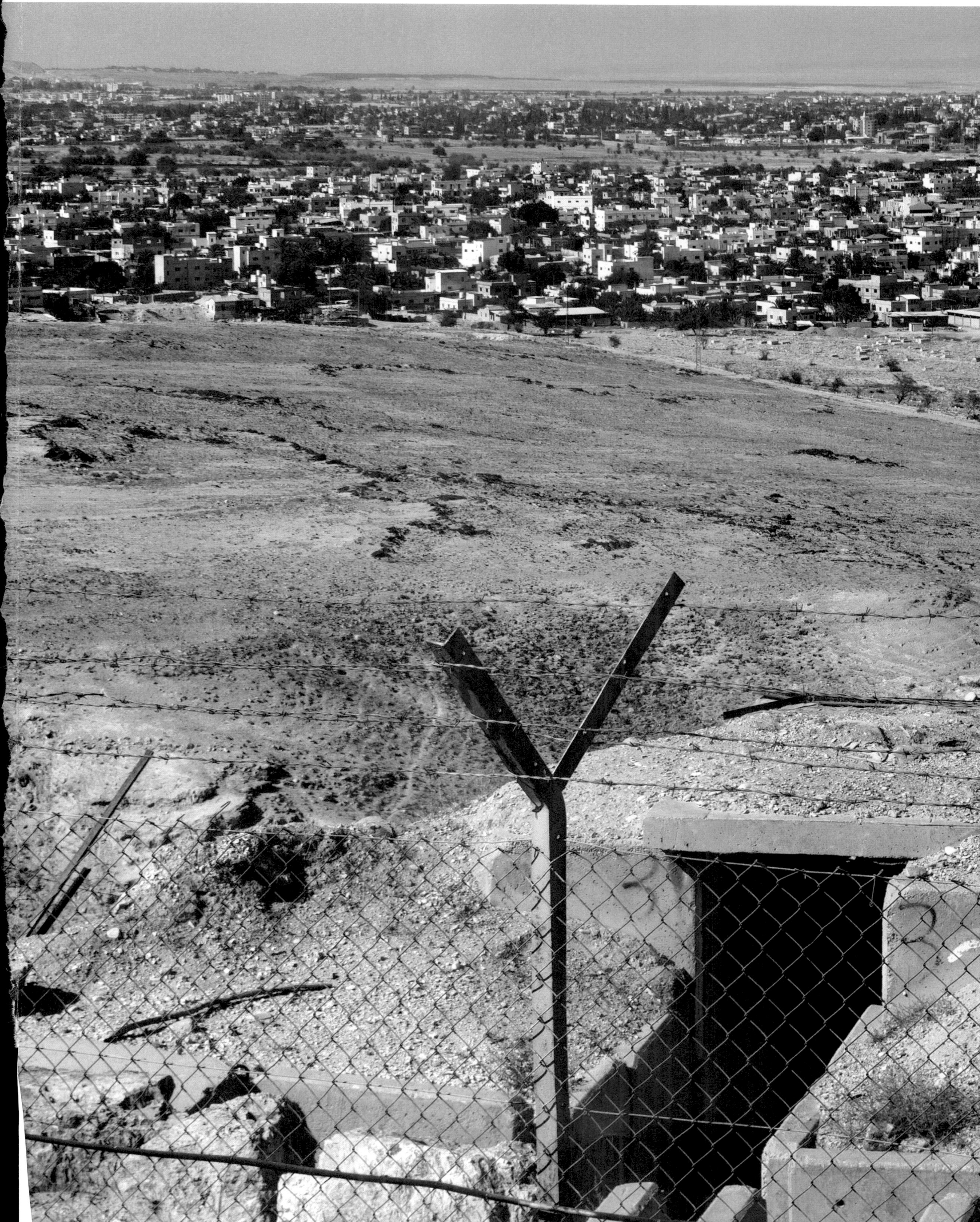

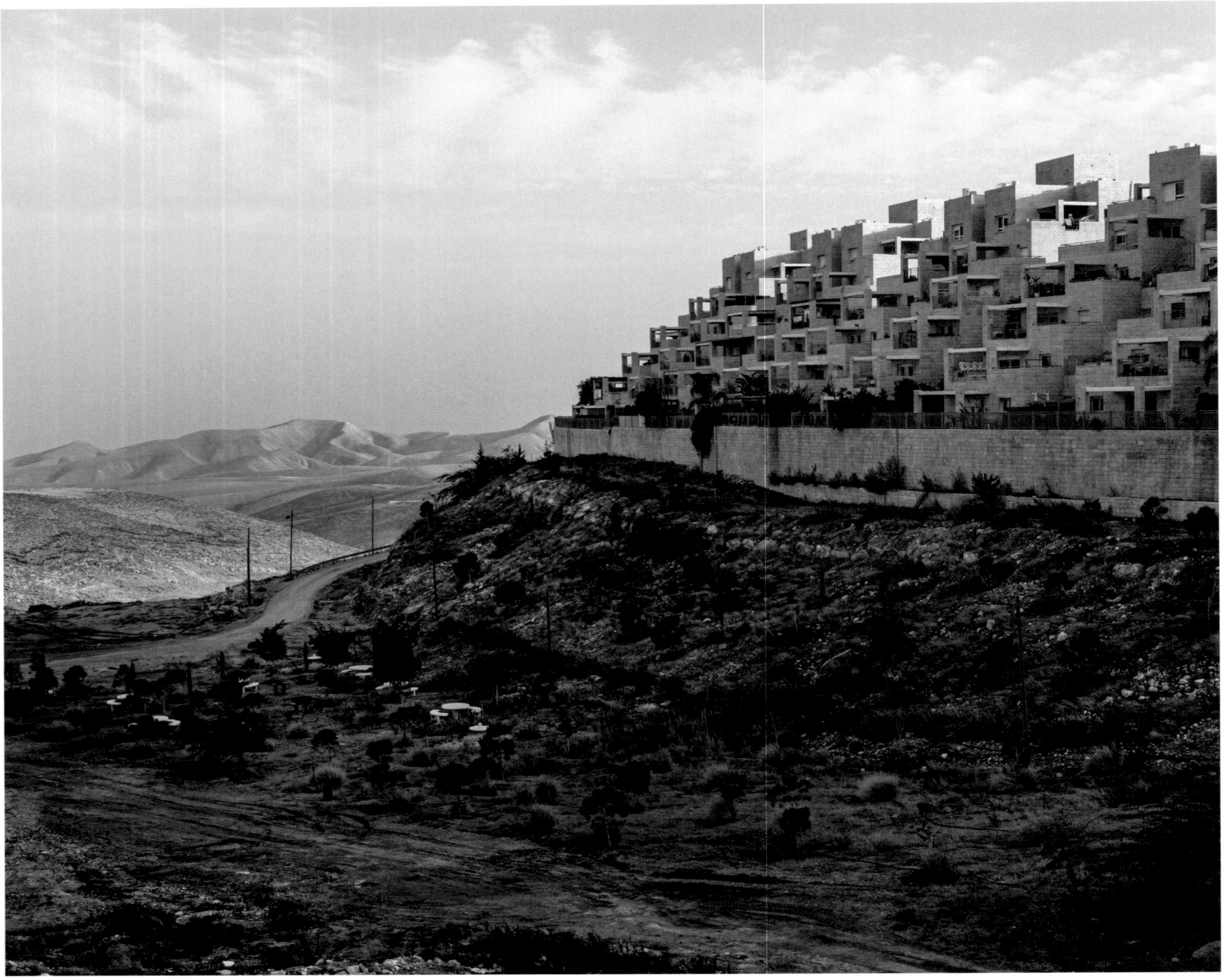

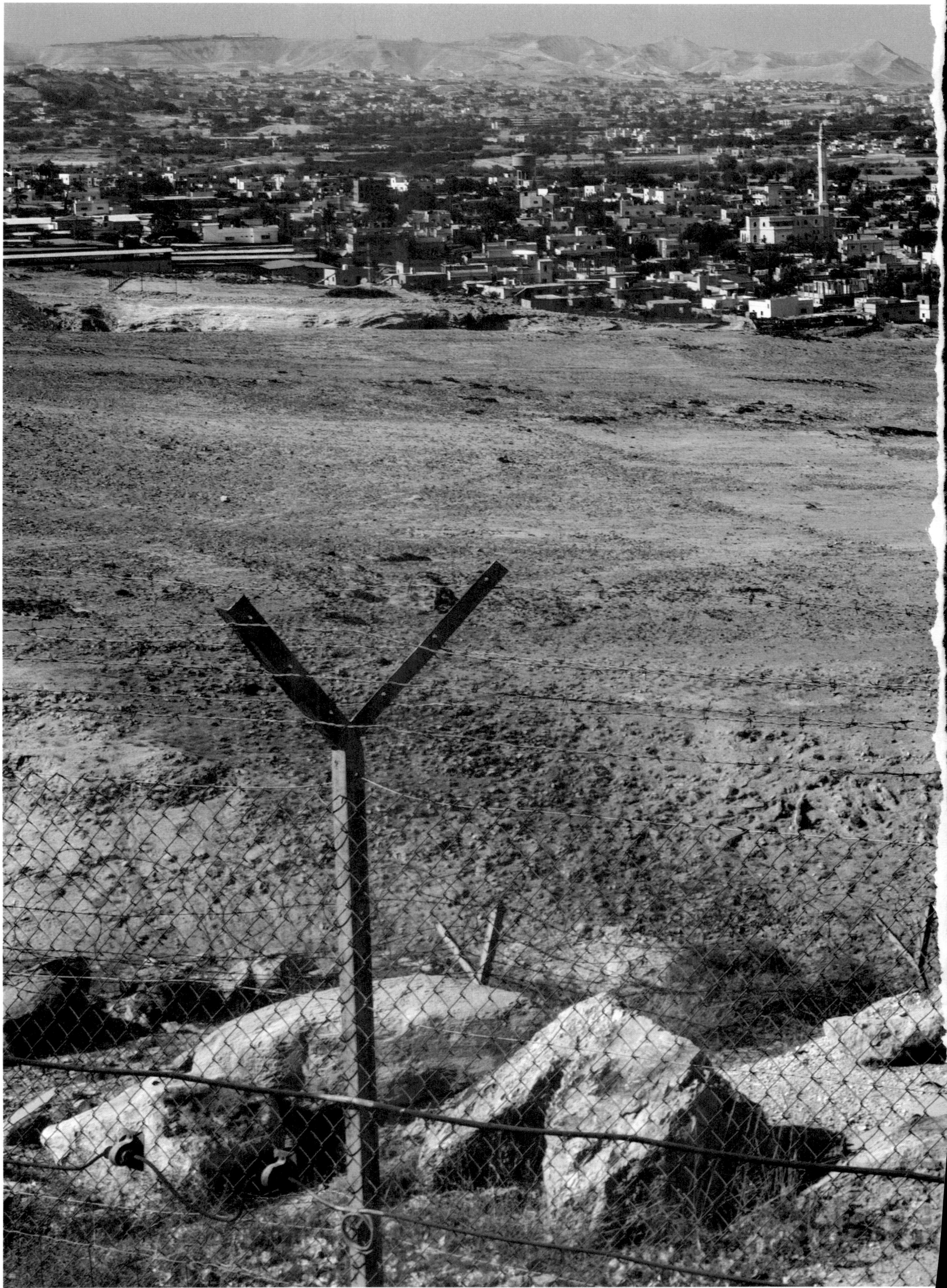

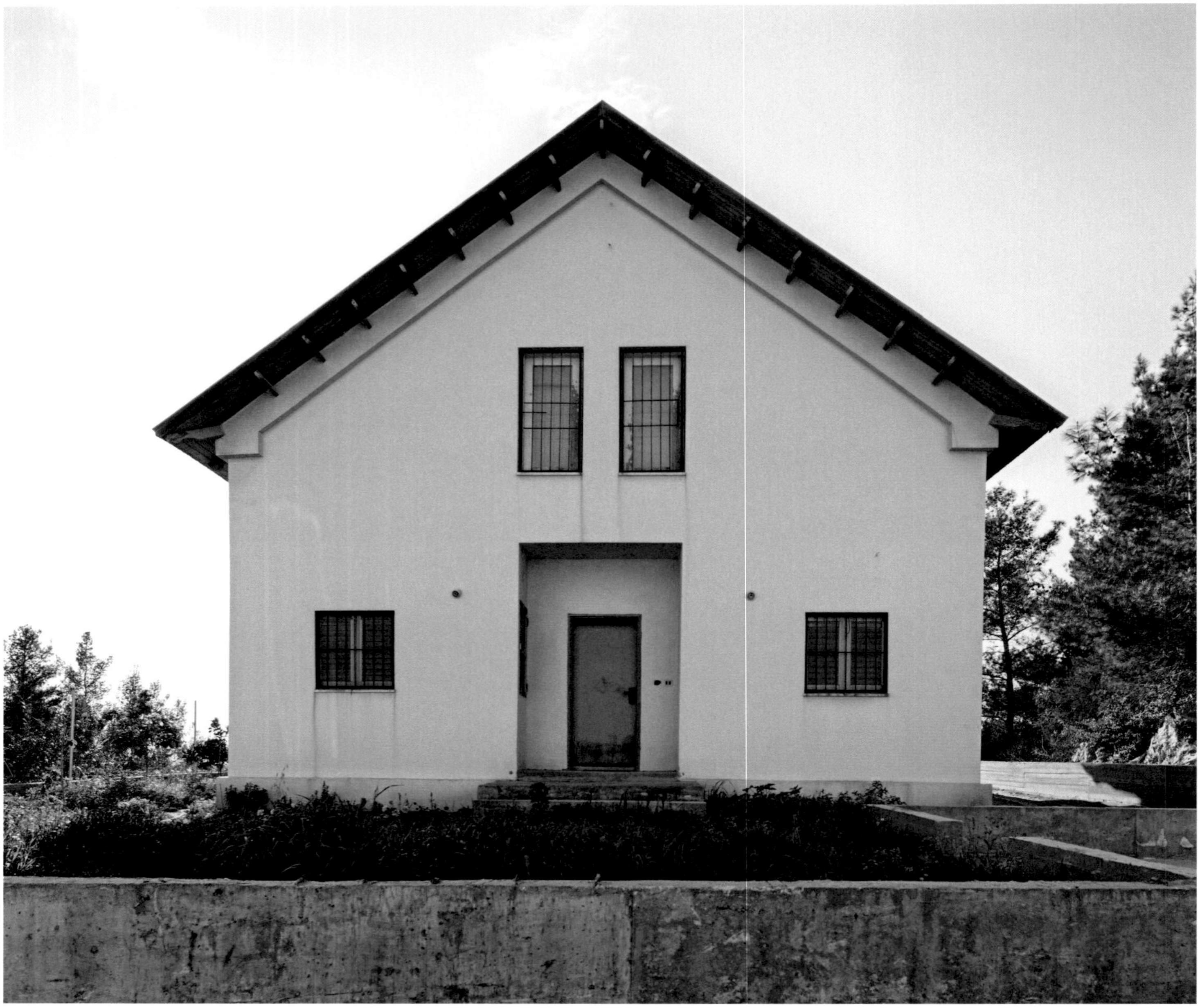

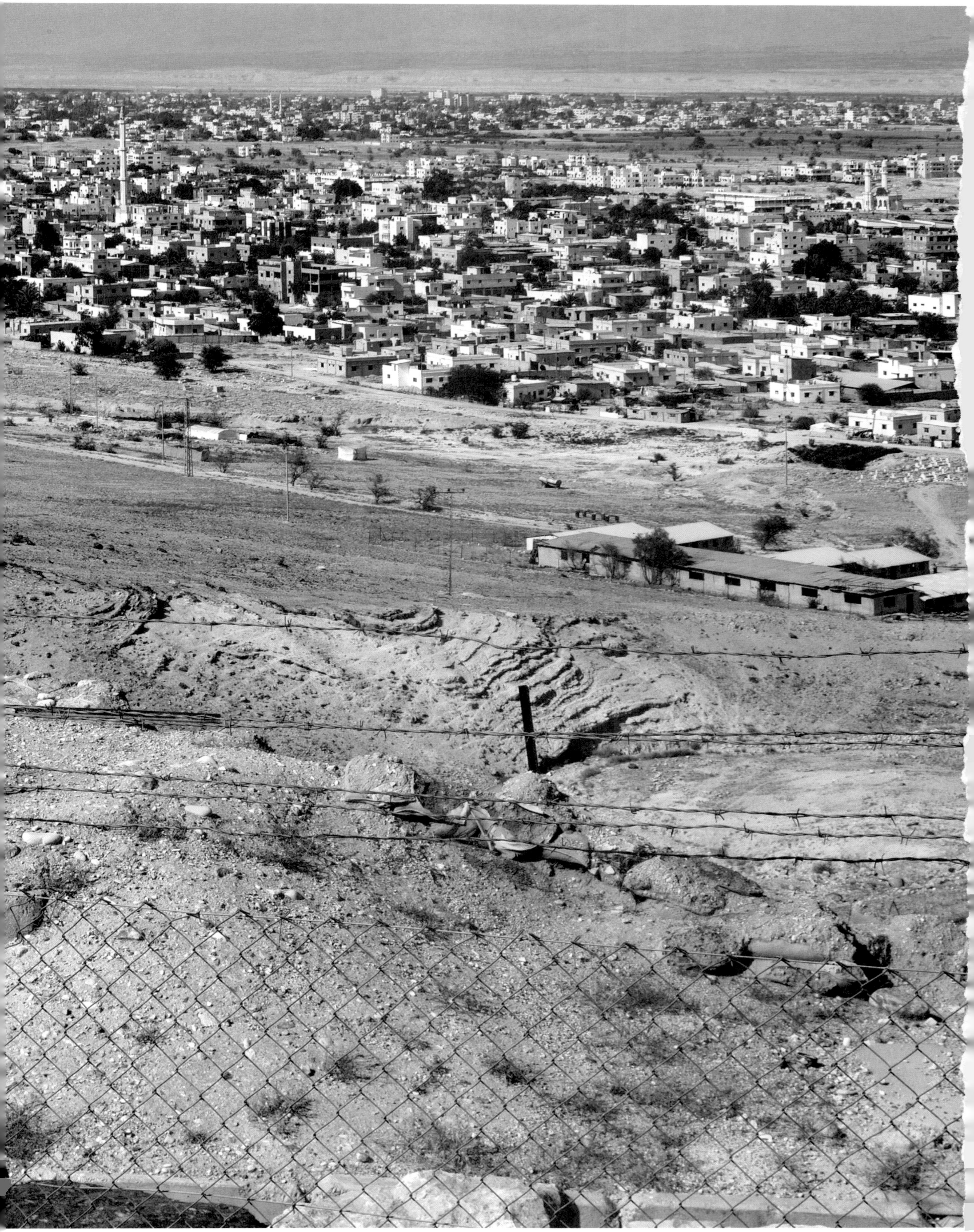

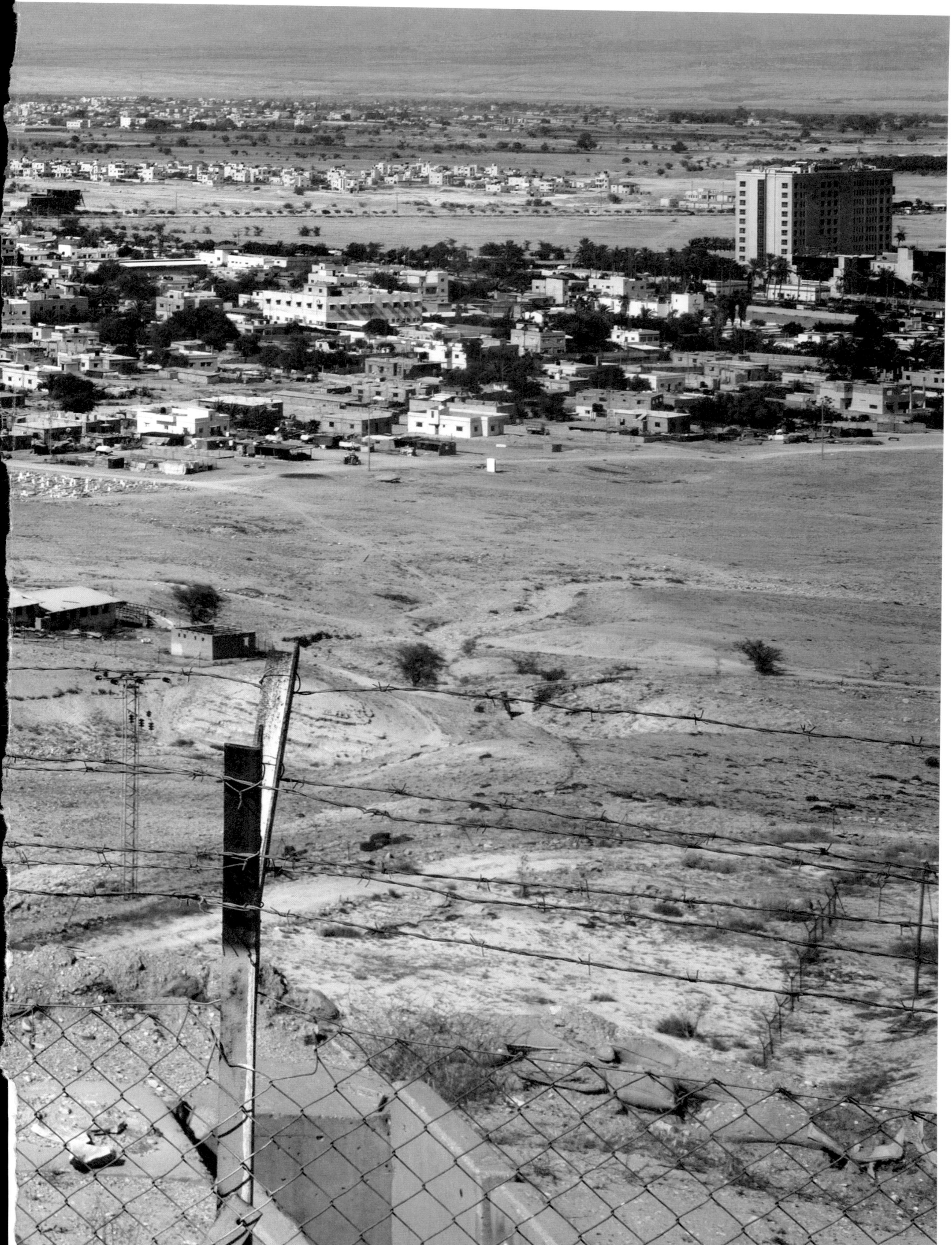

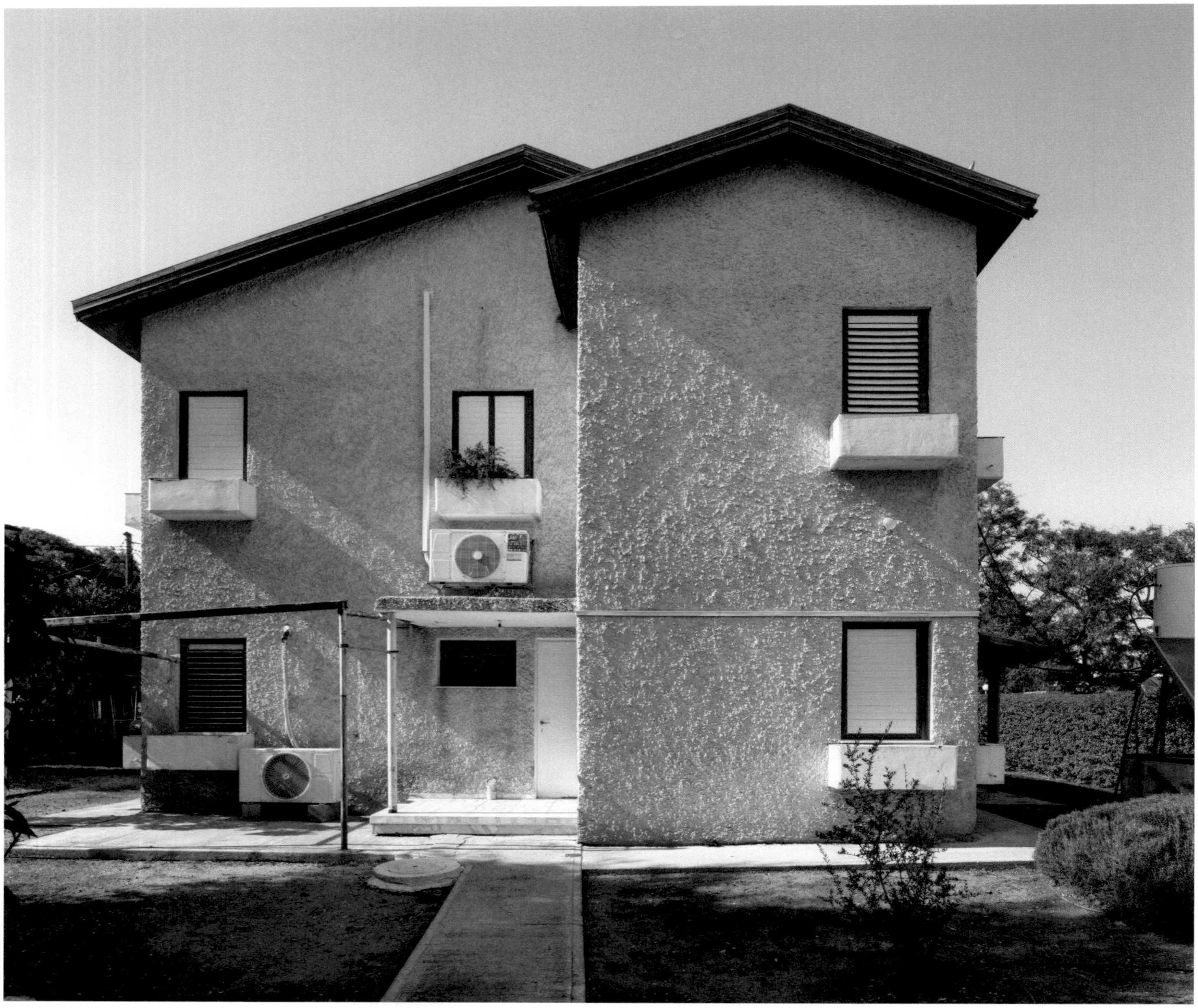

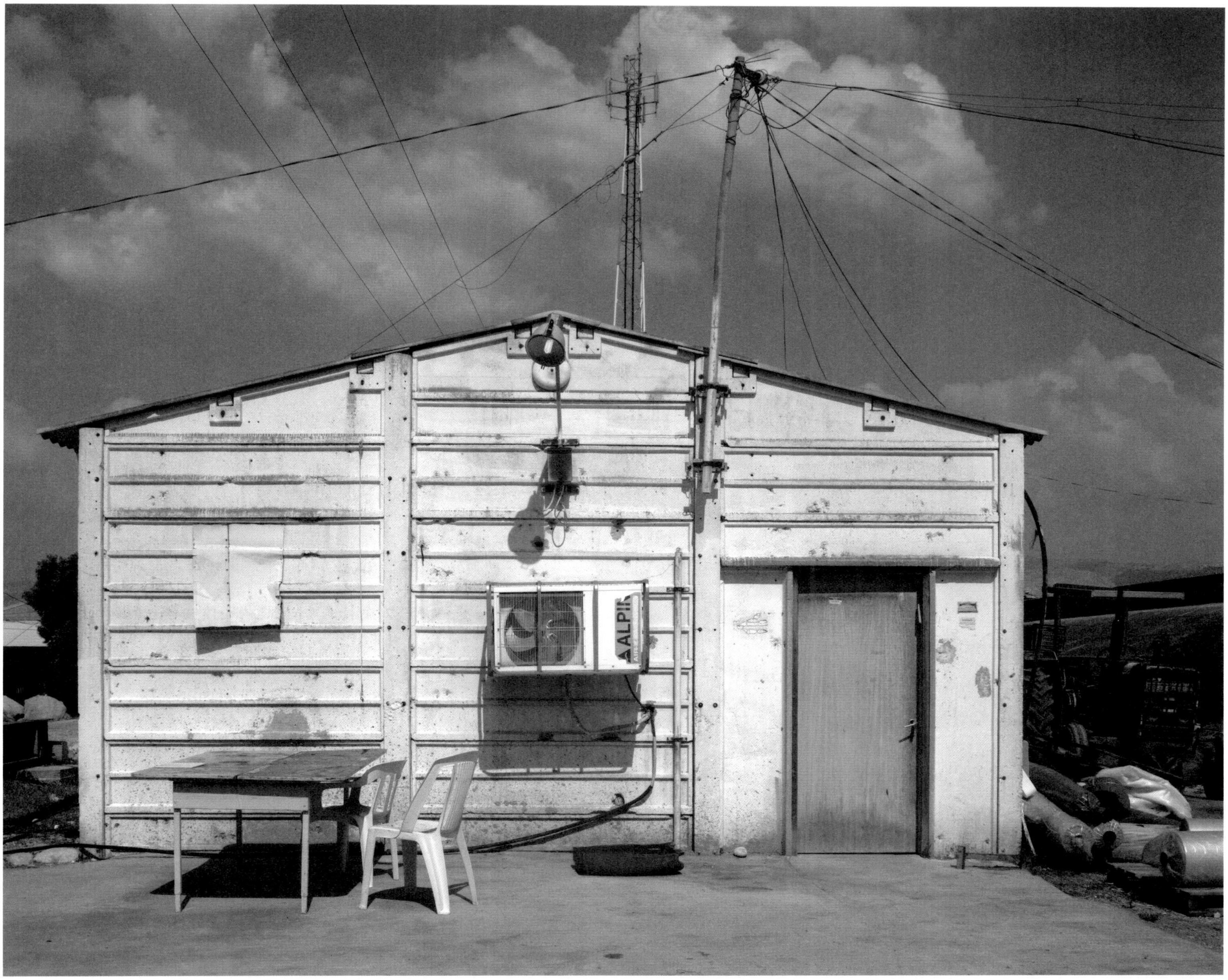
ALPI

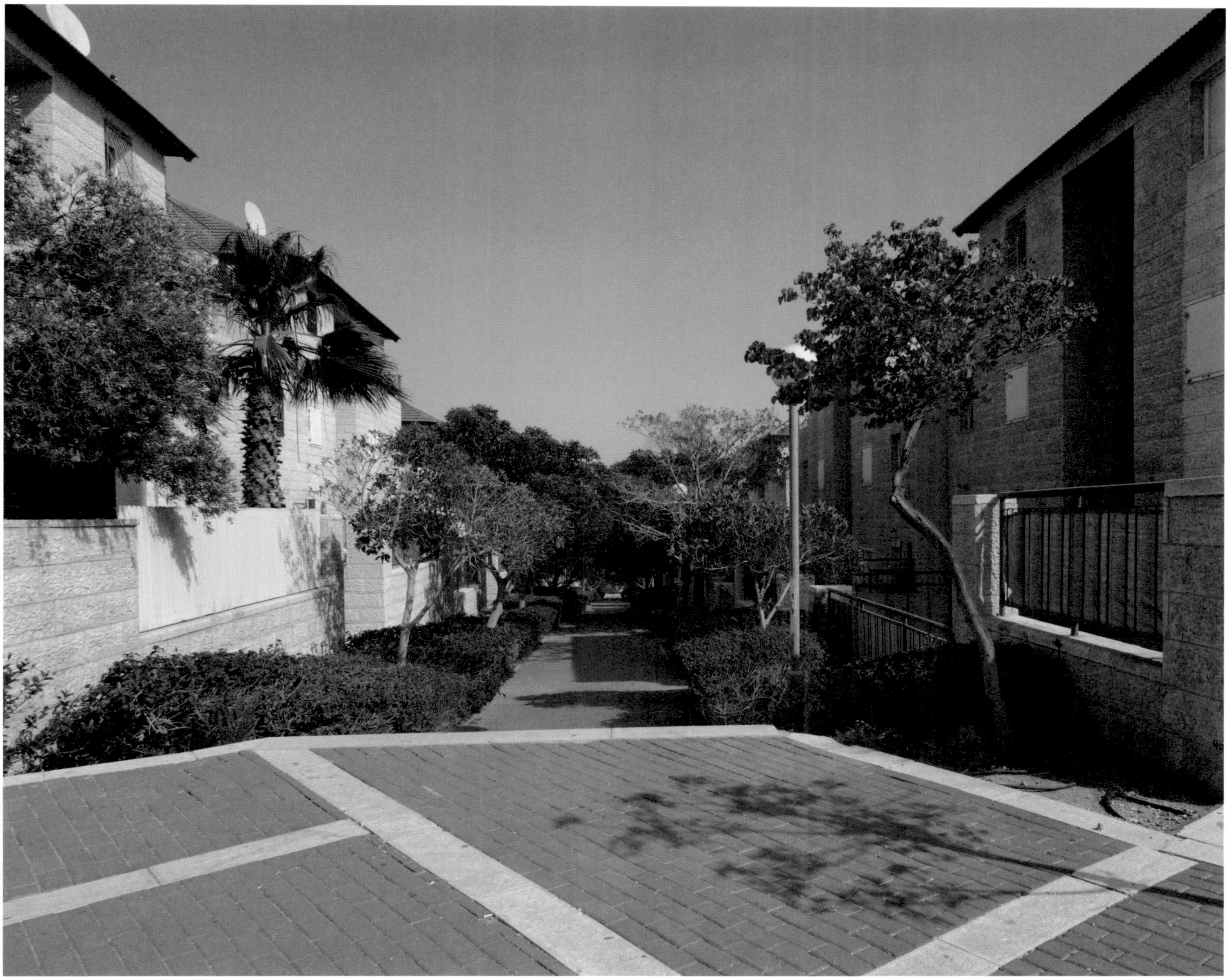

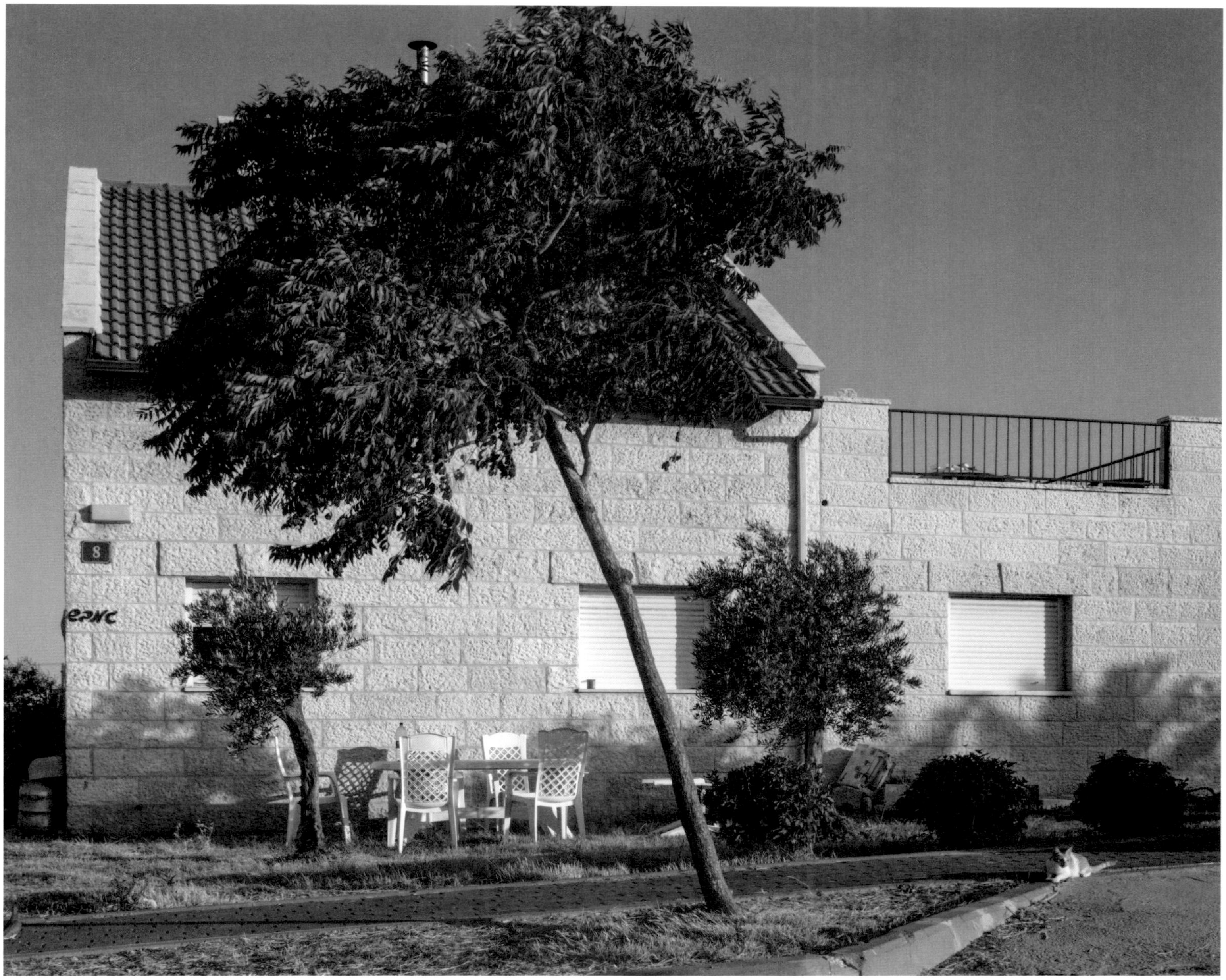
8

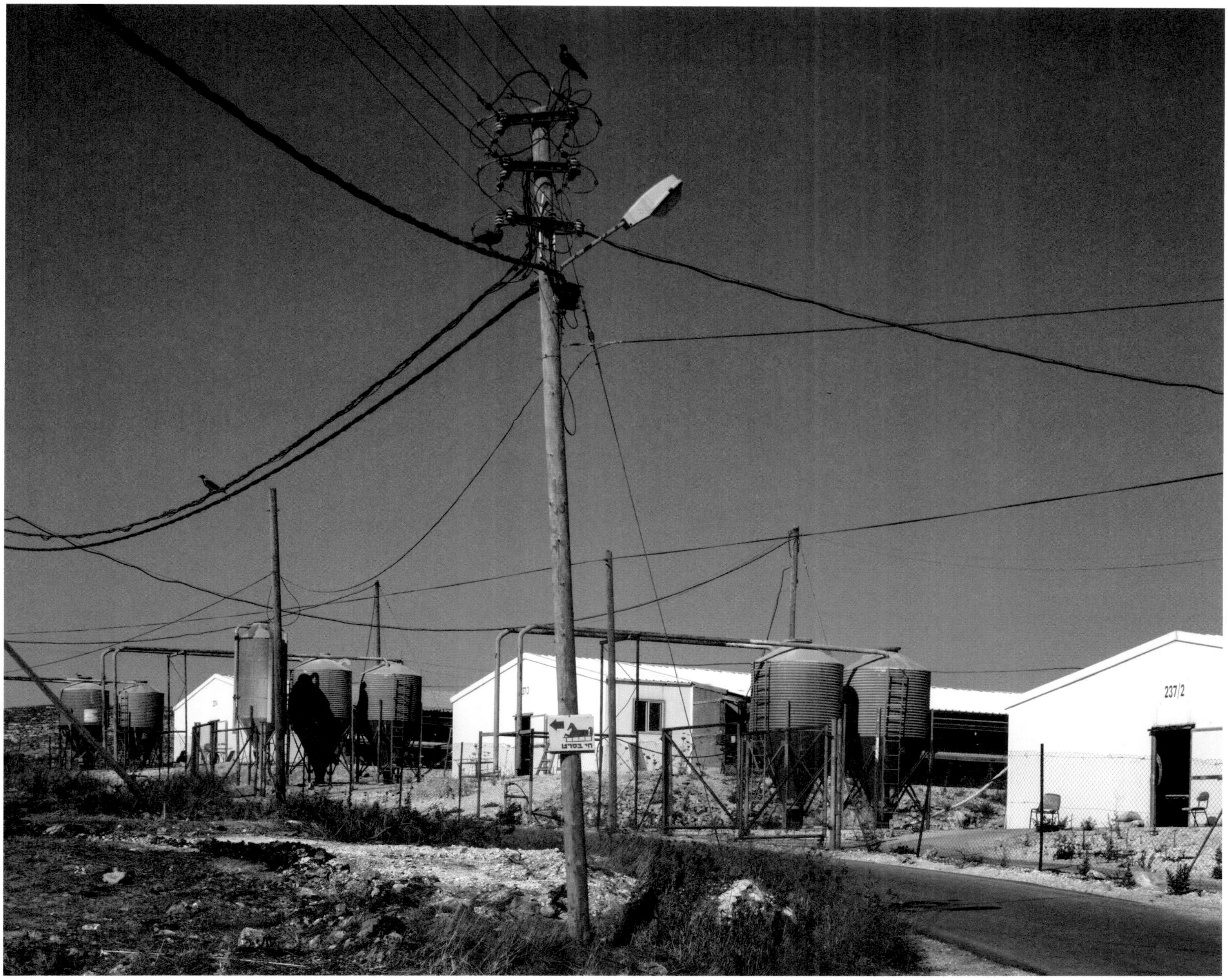
237/2

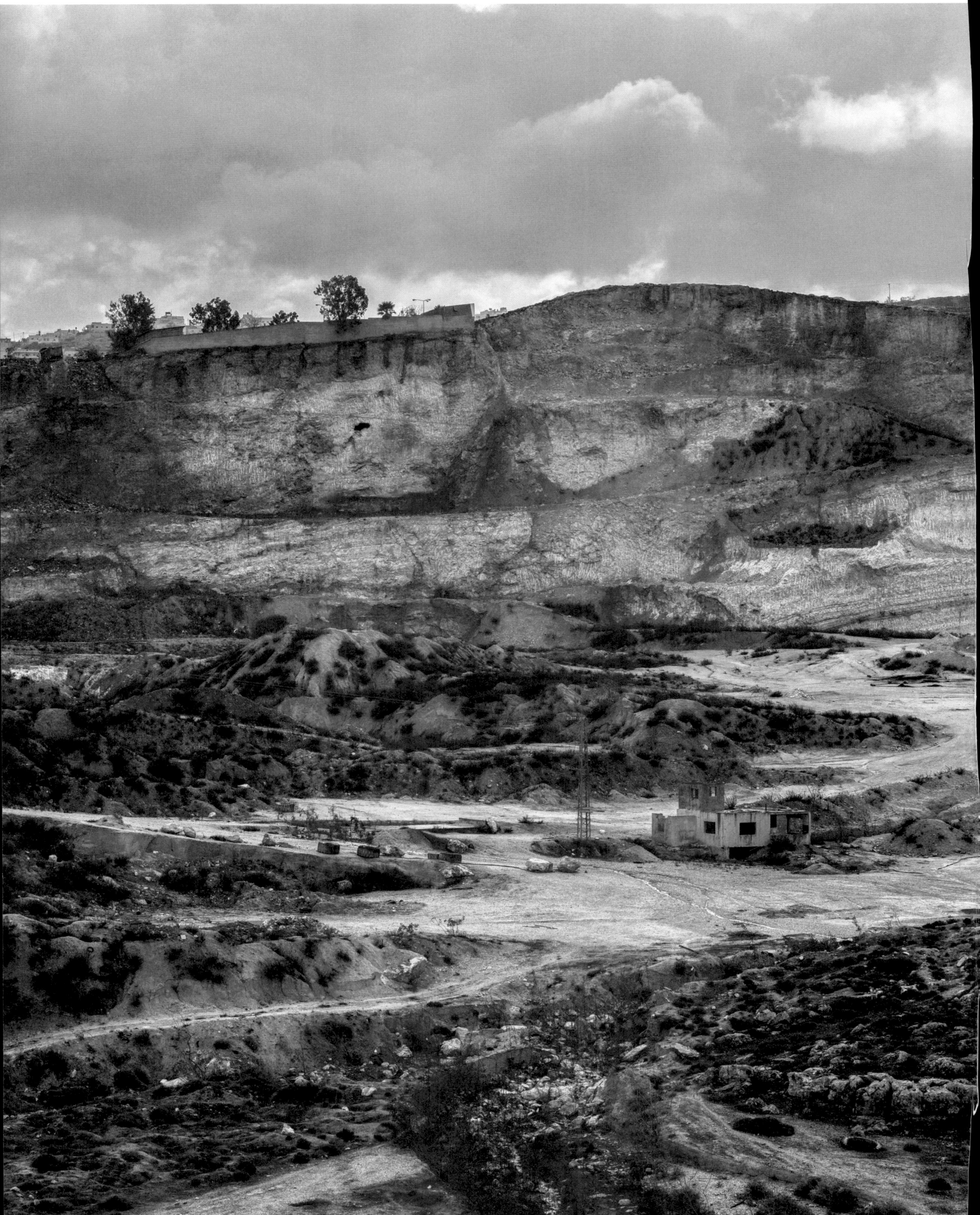

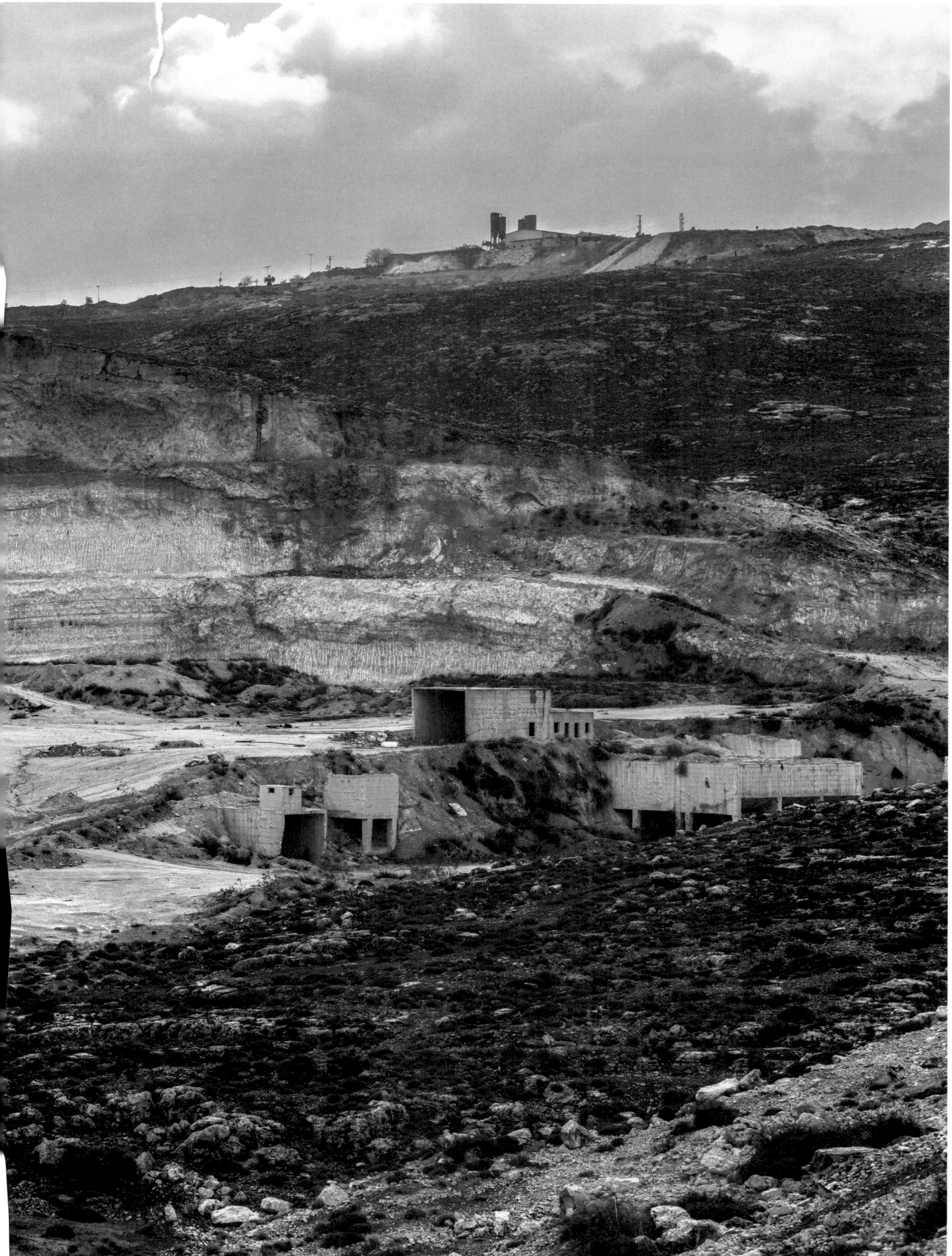

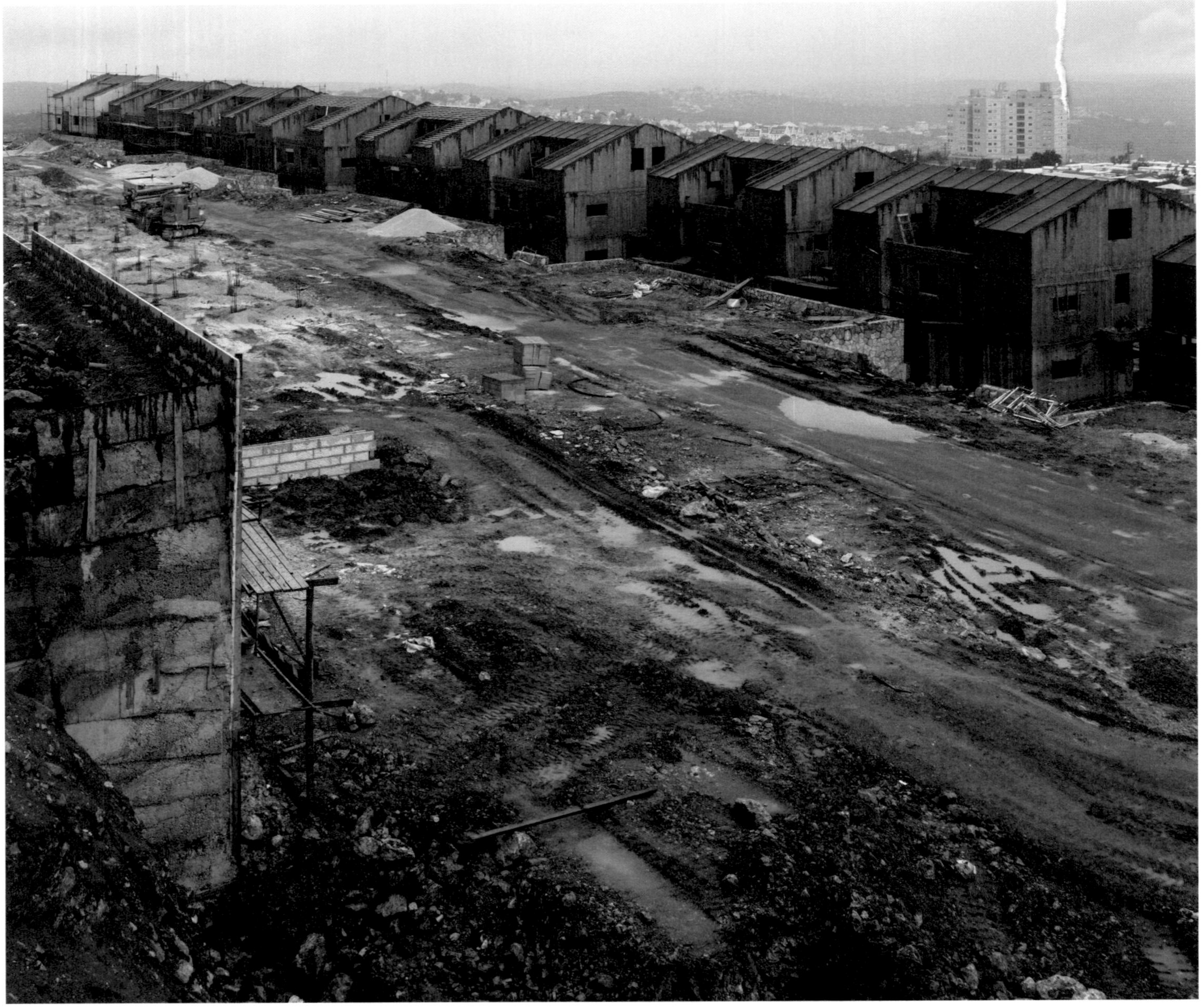

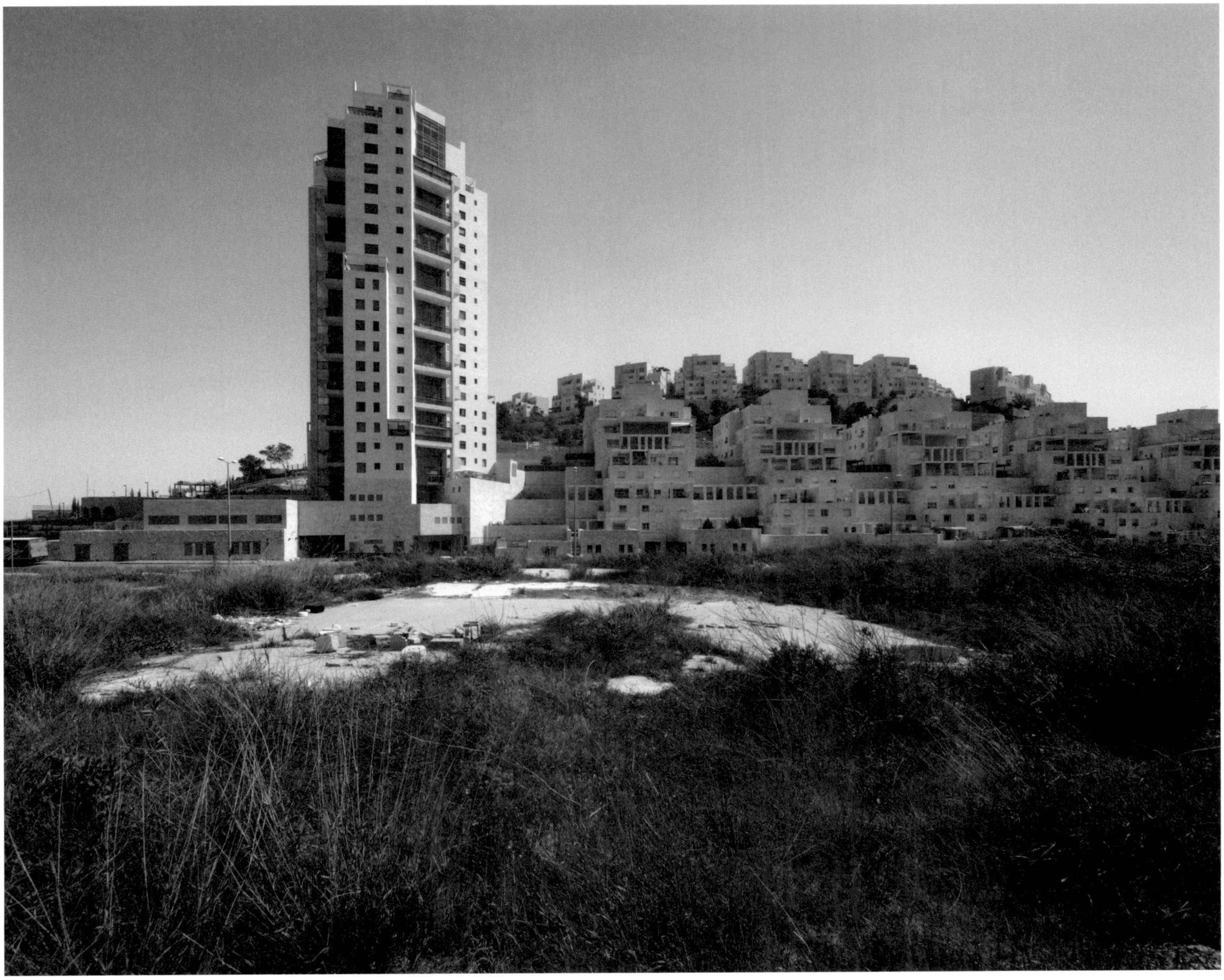

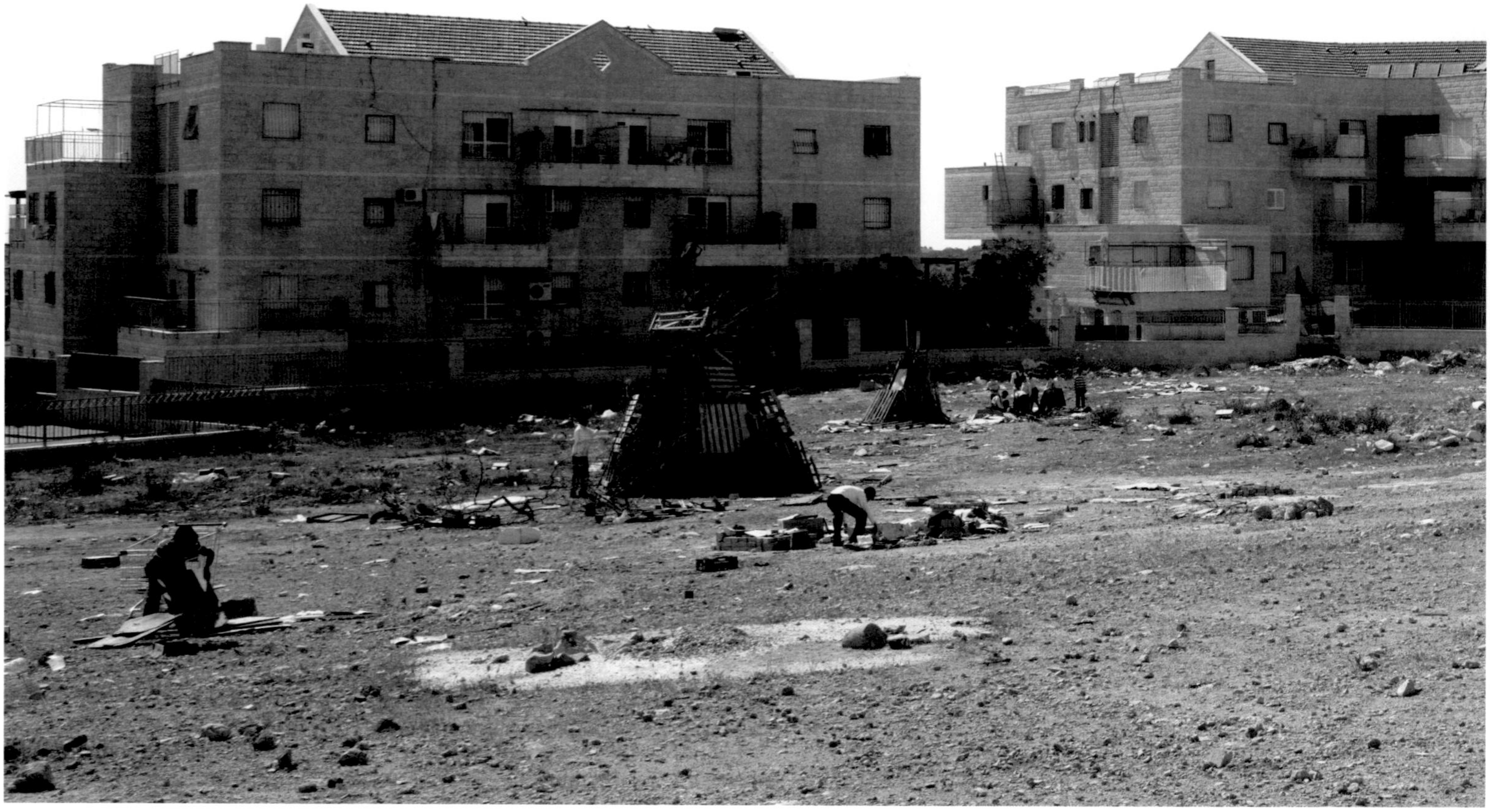

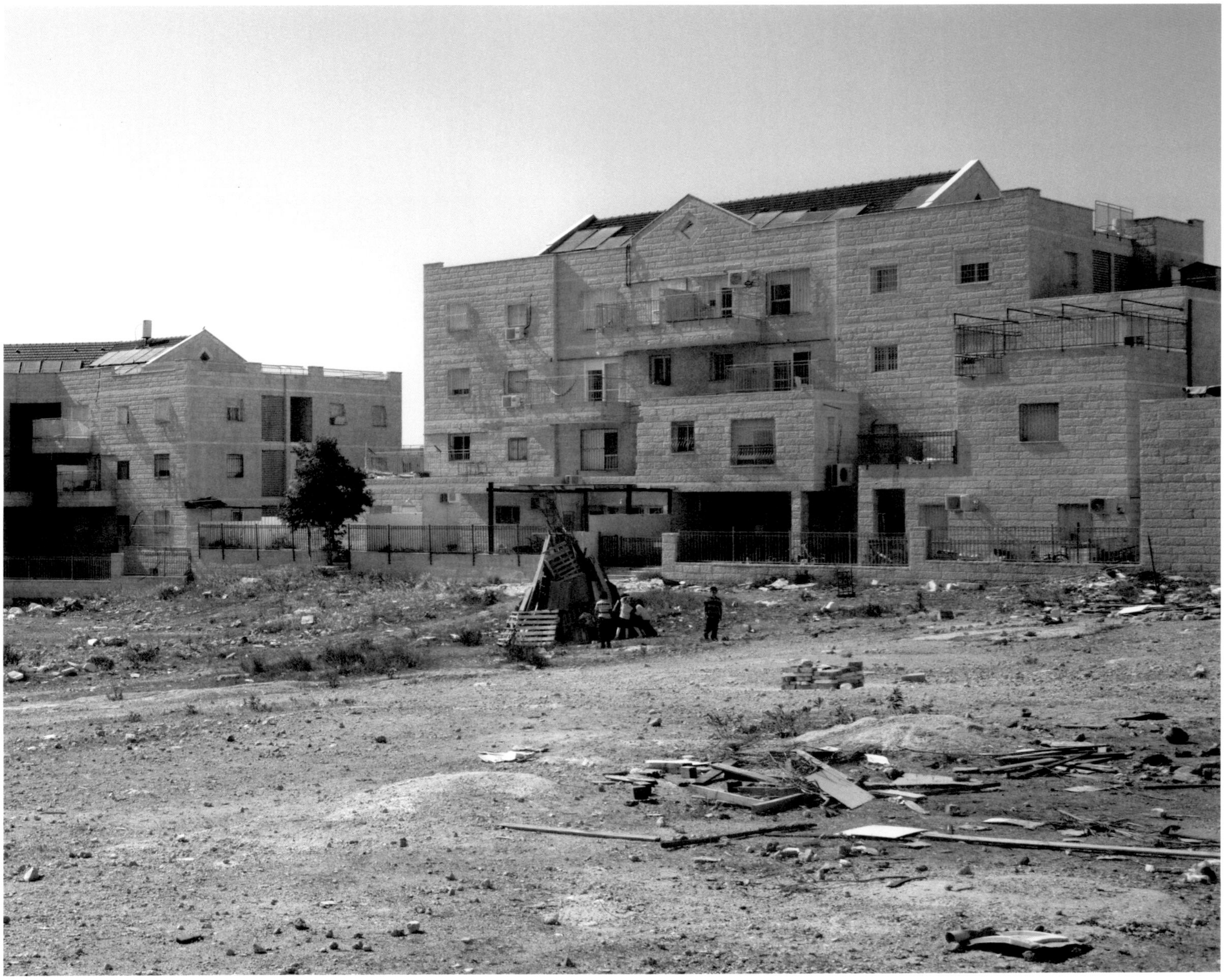

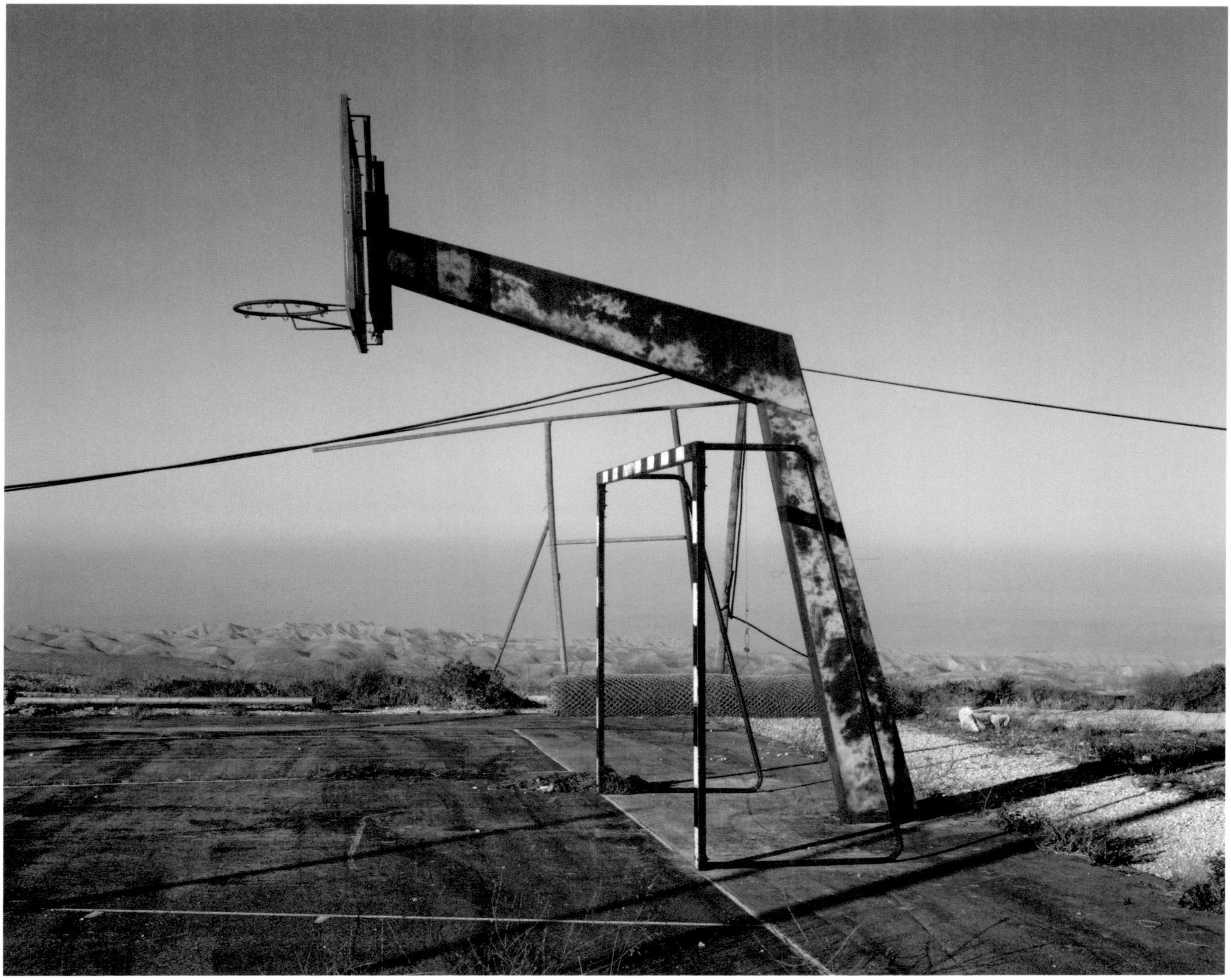

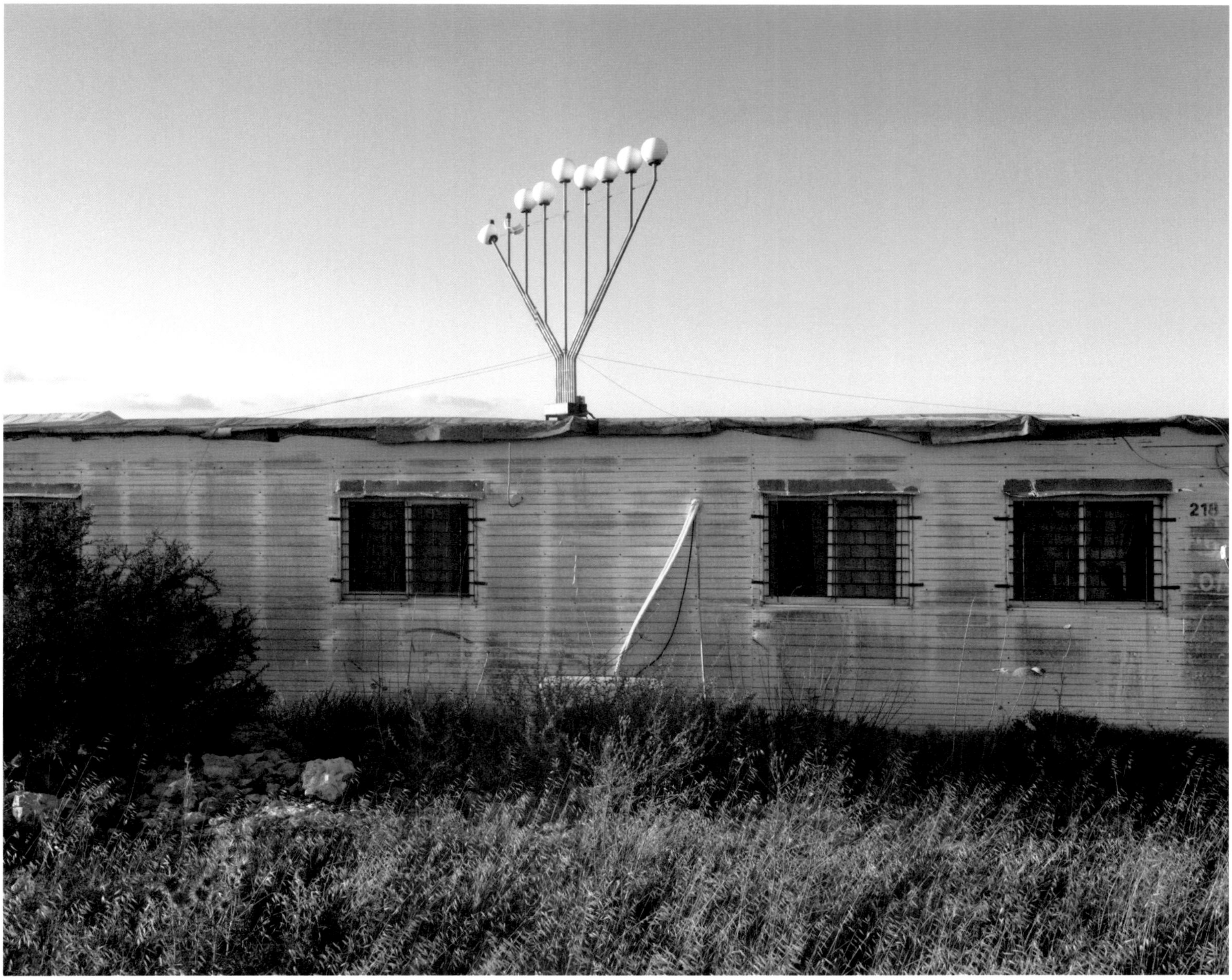
218

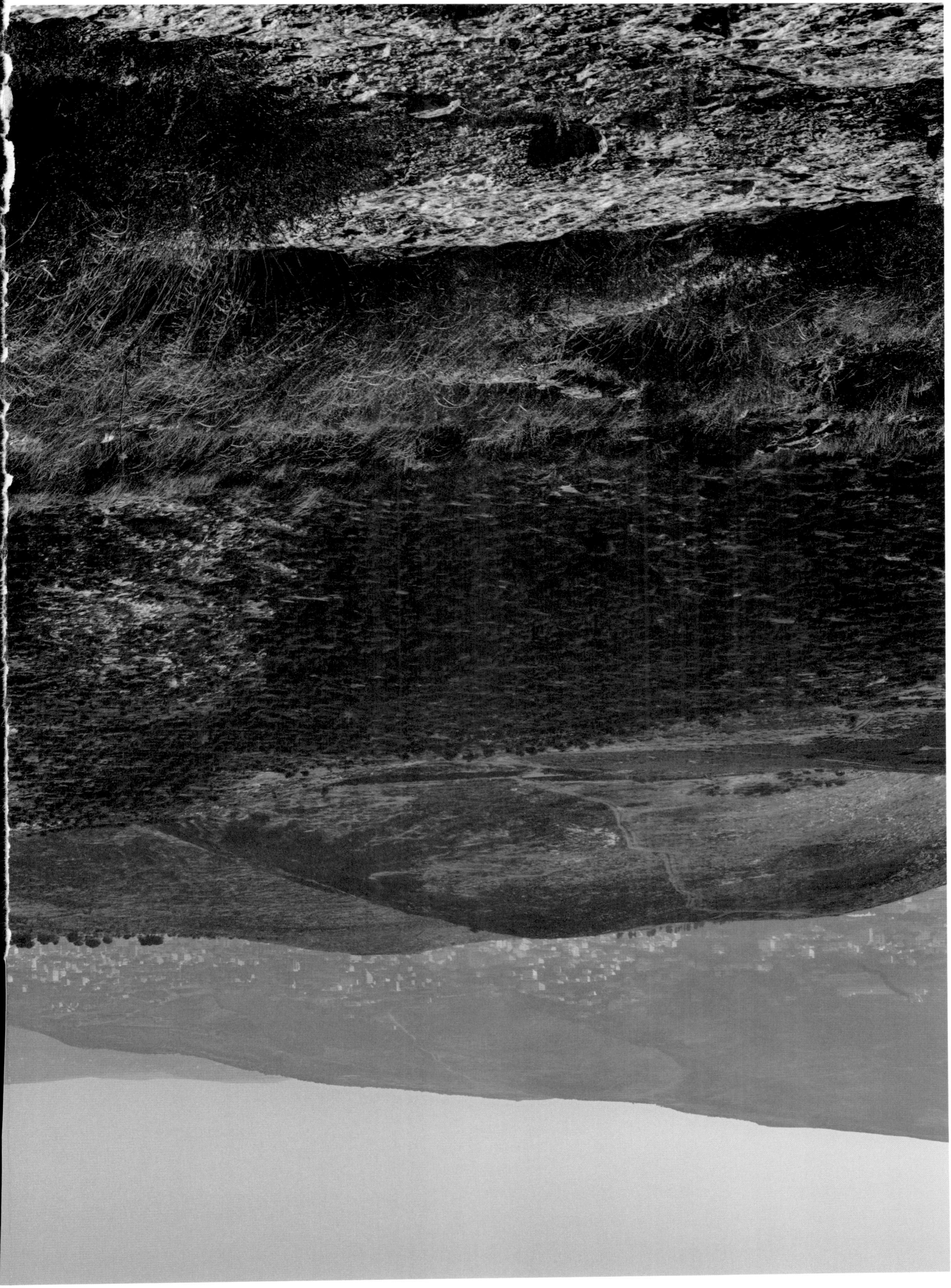

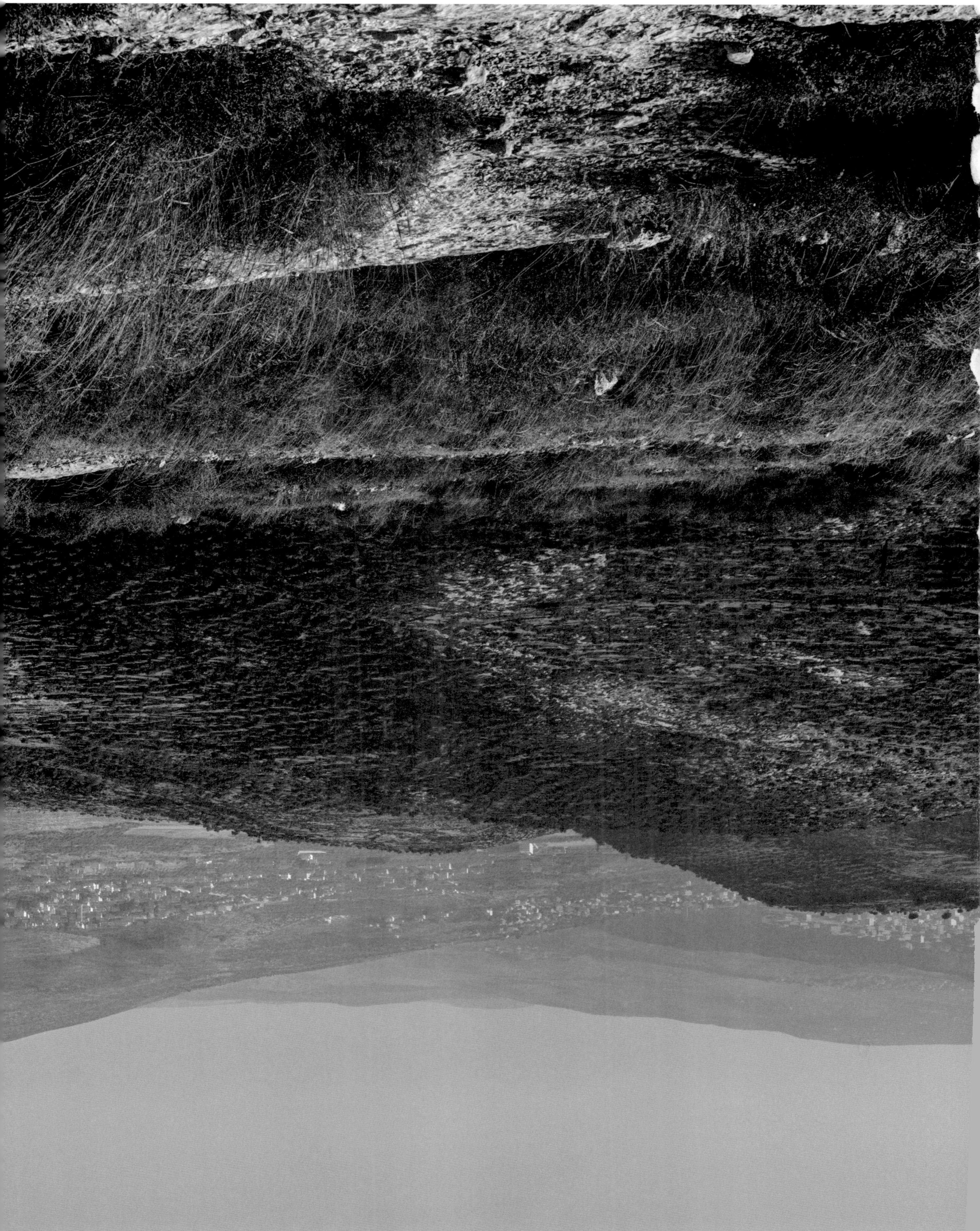

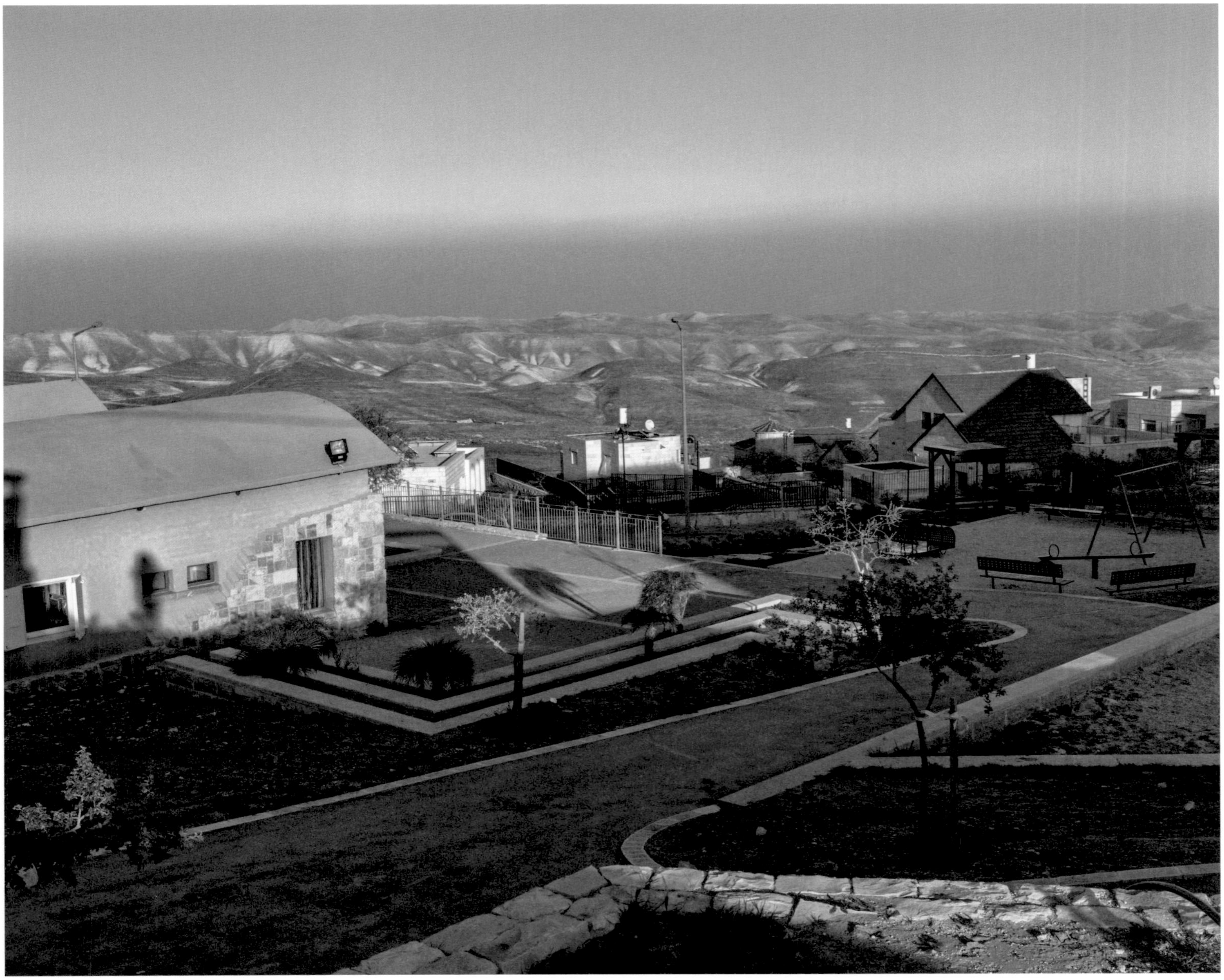

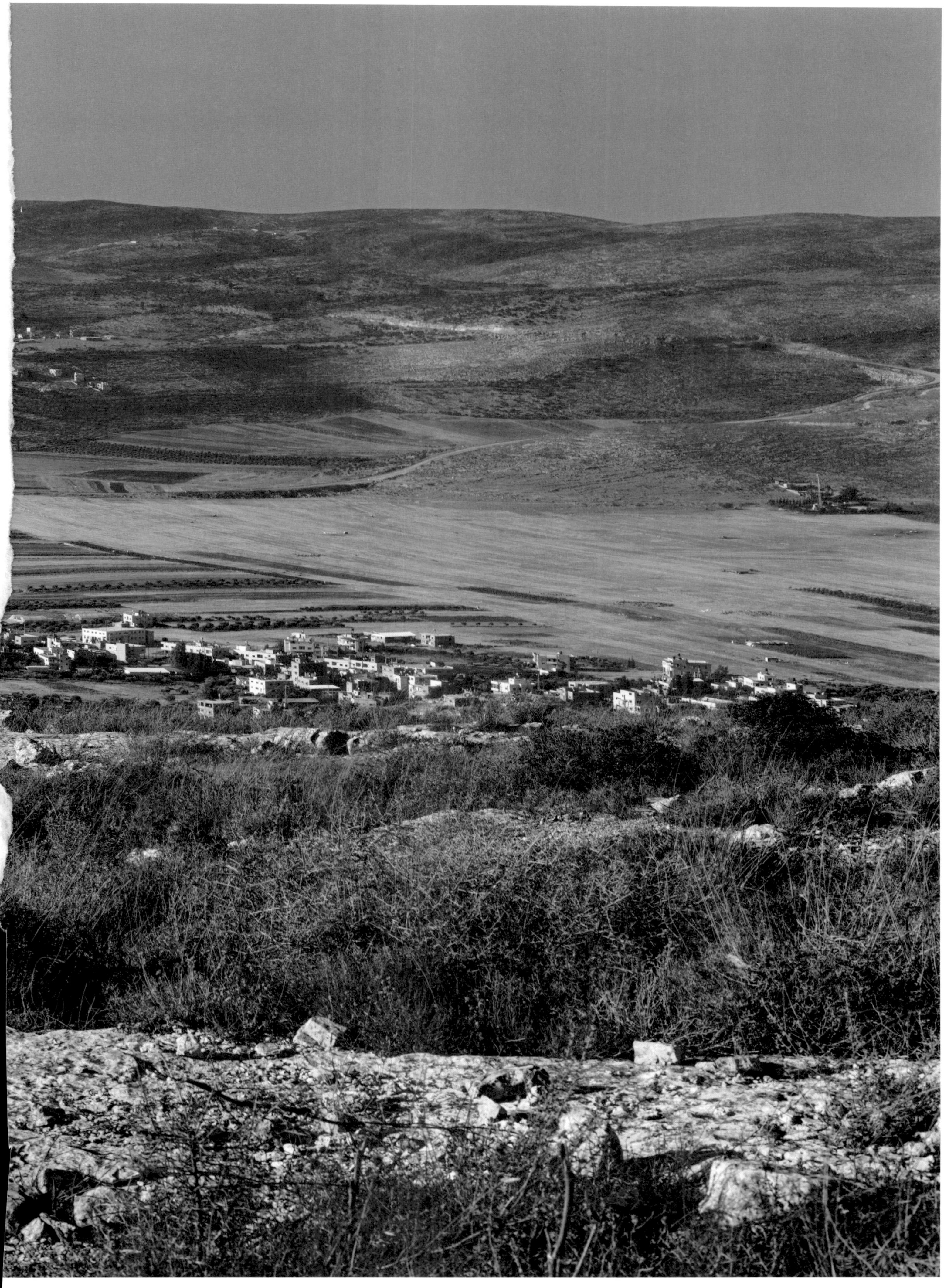

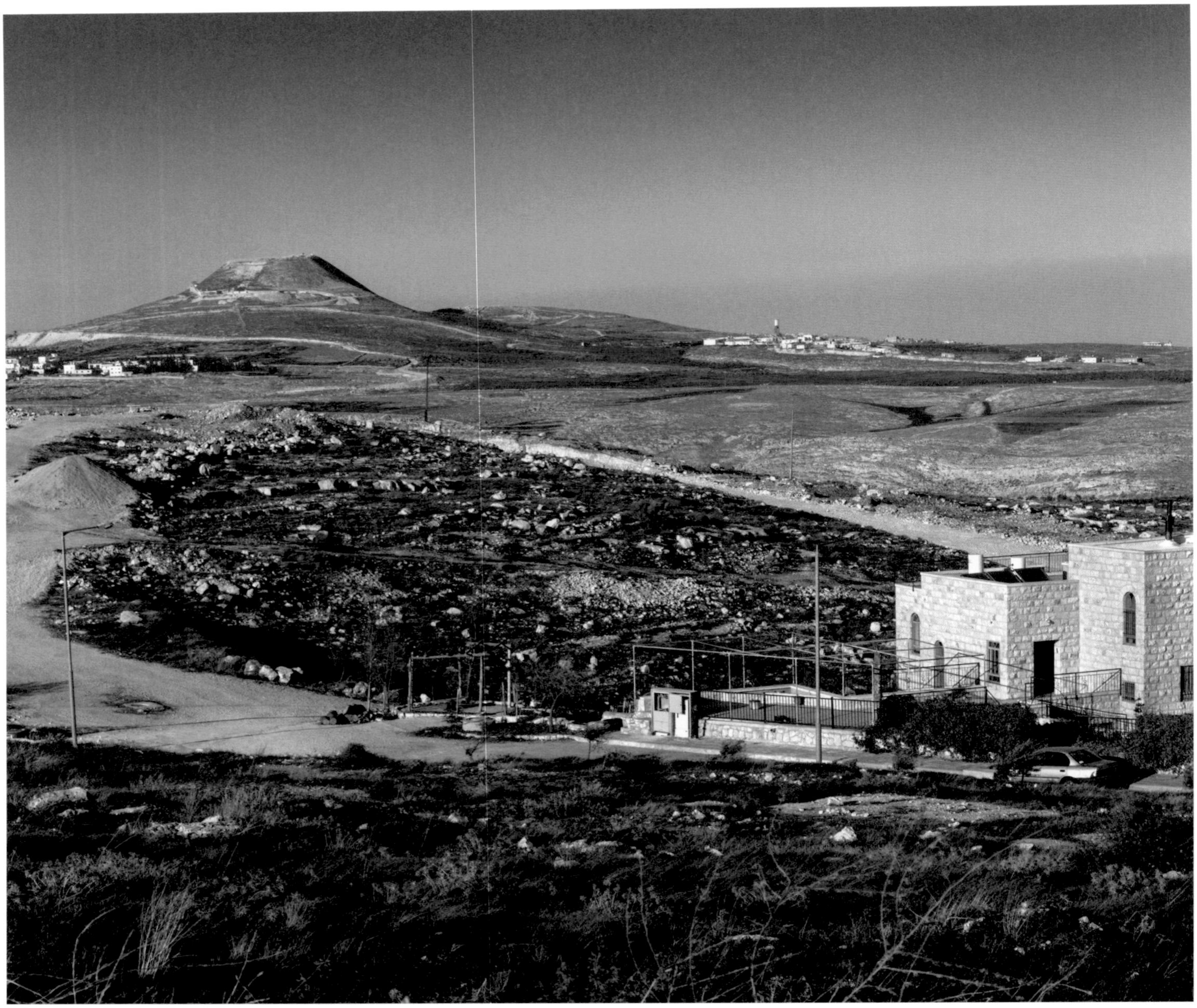

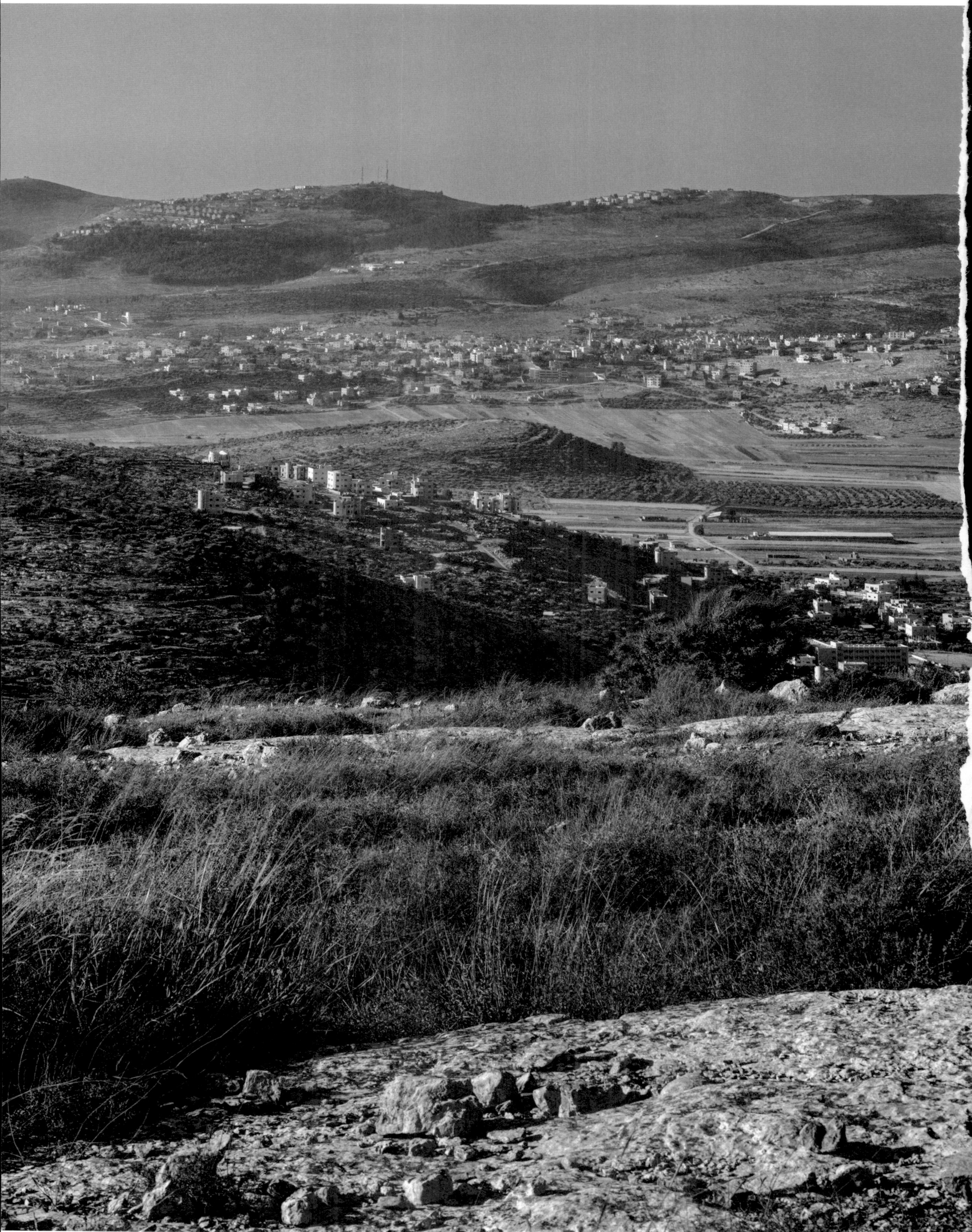

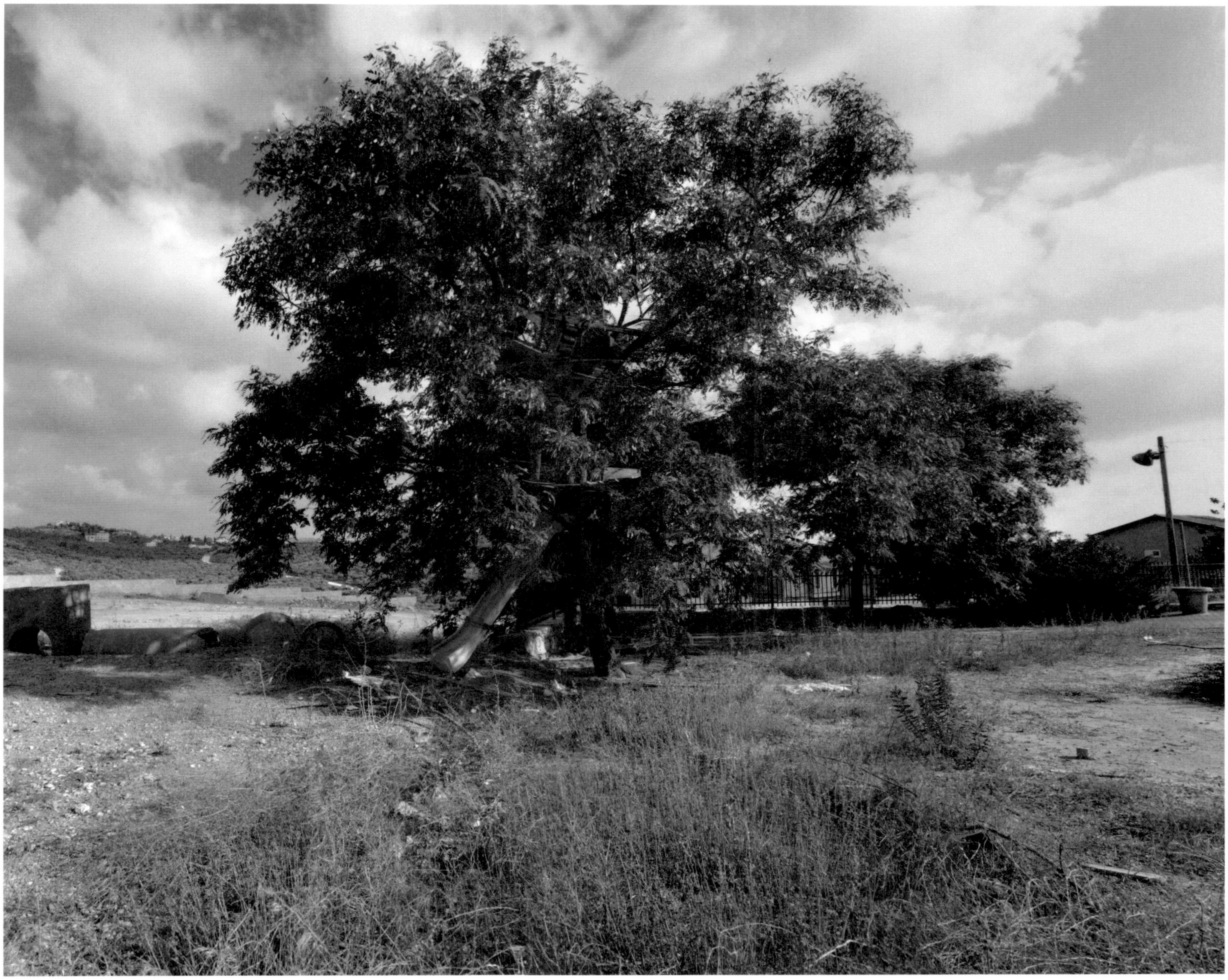

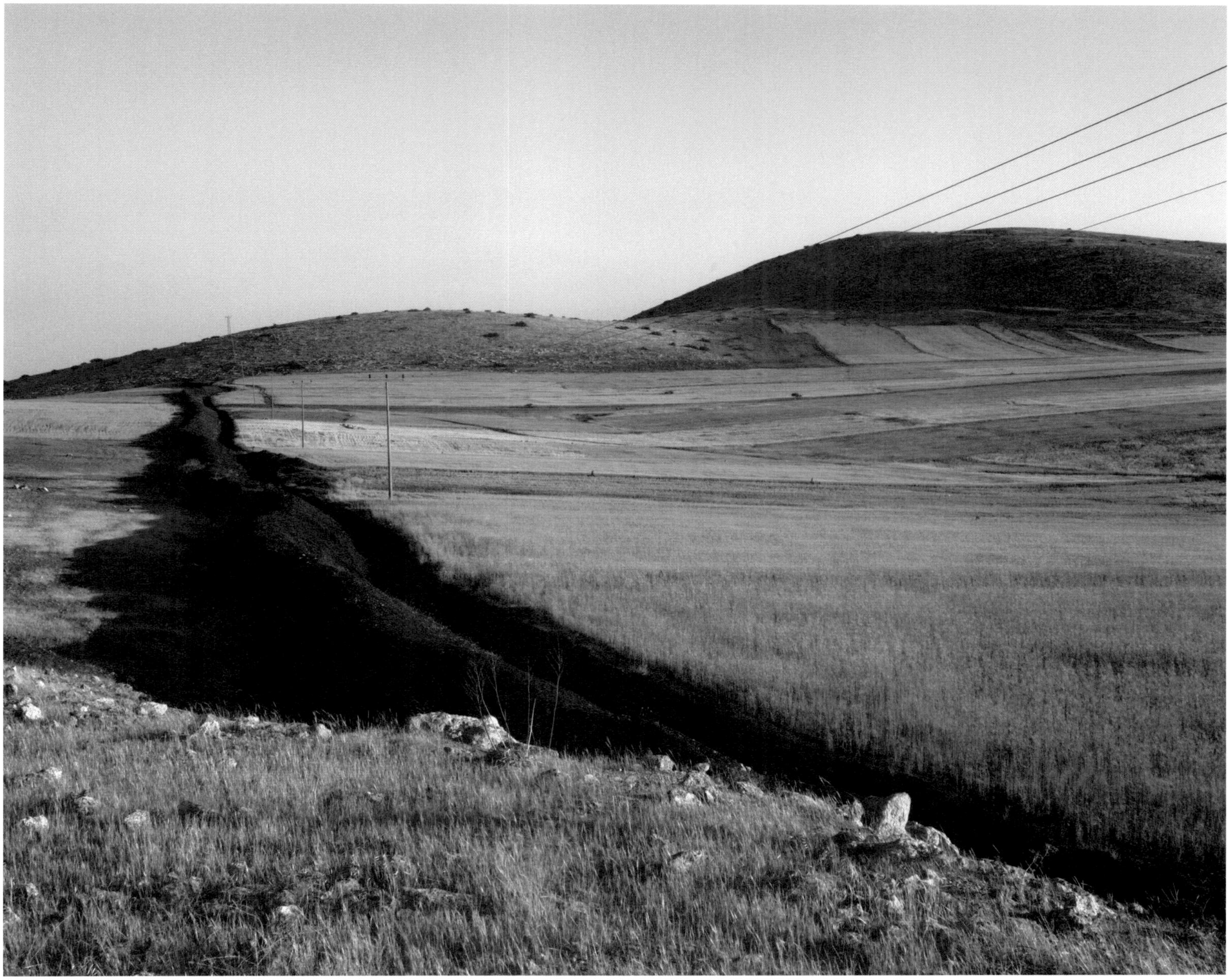

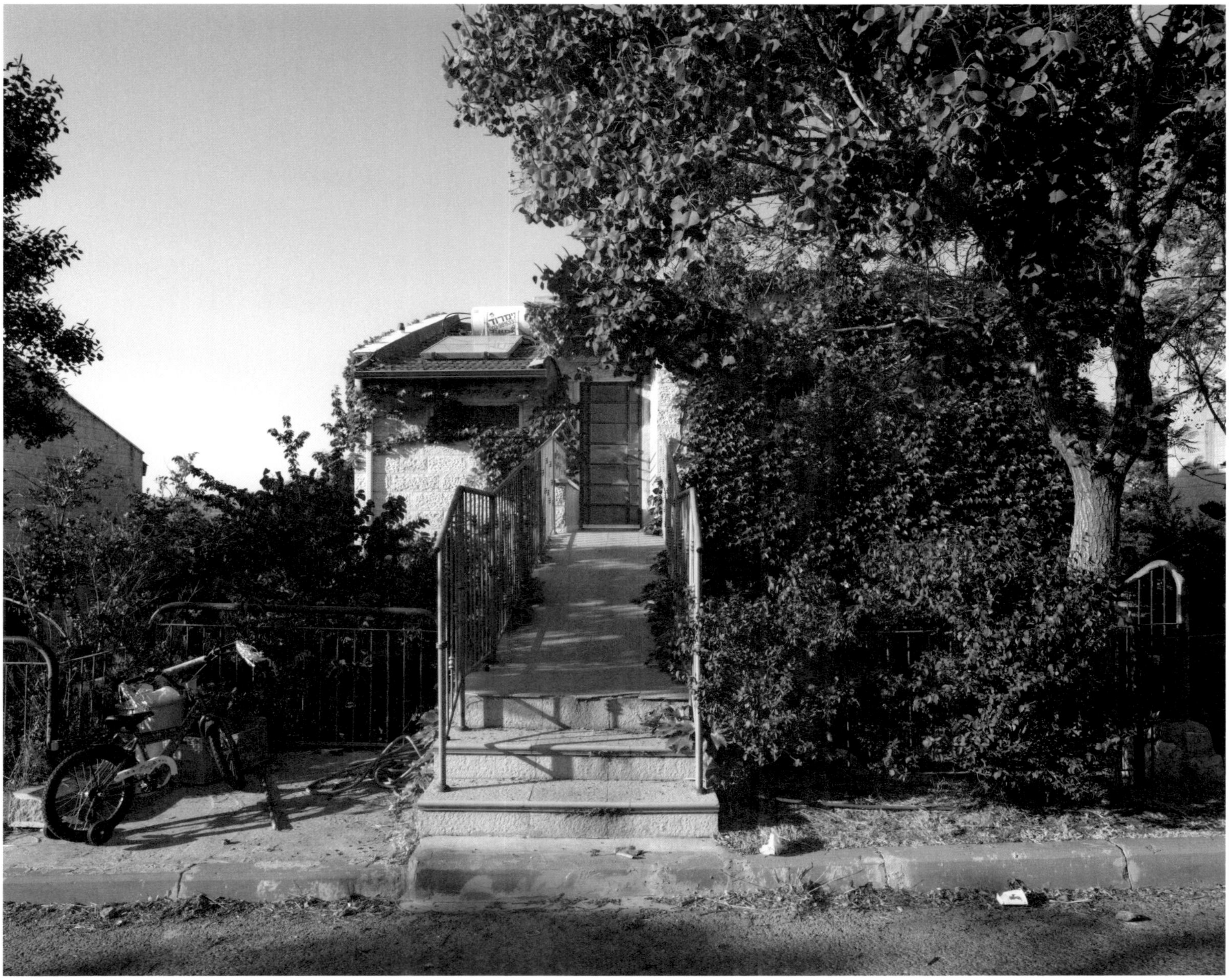

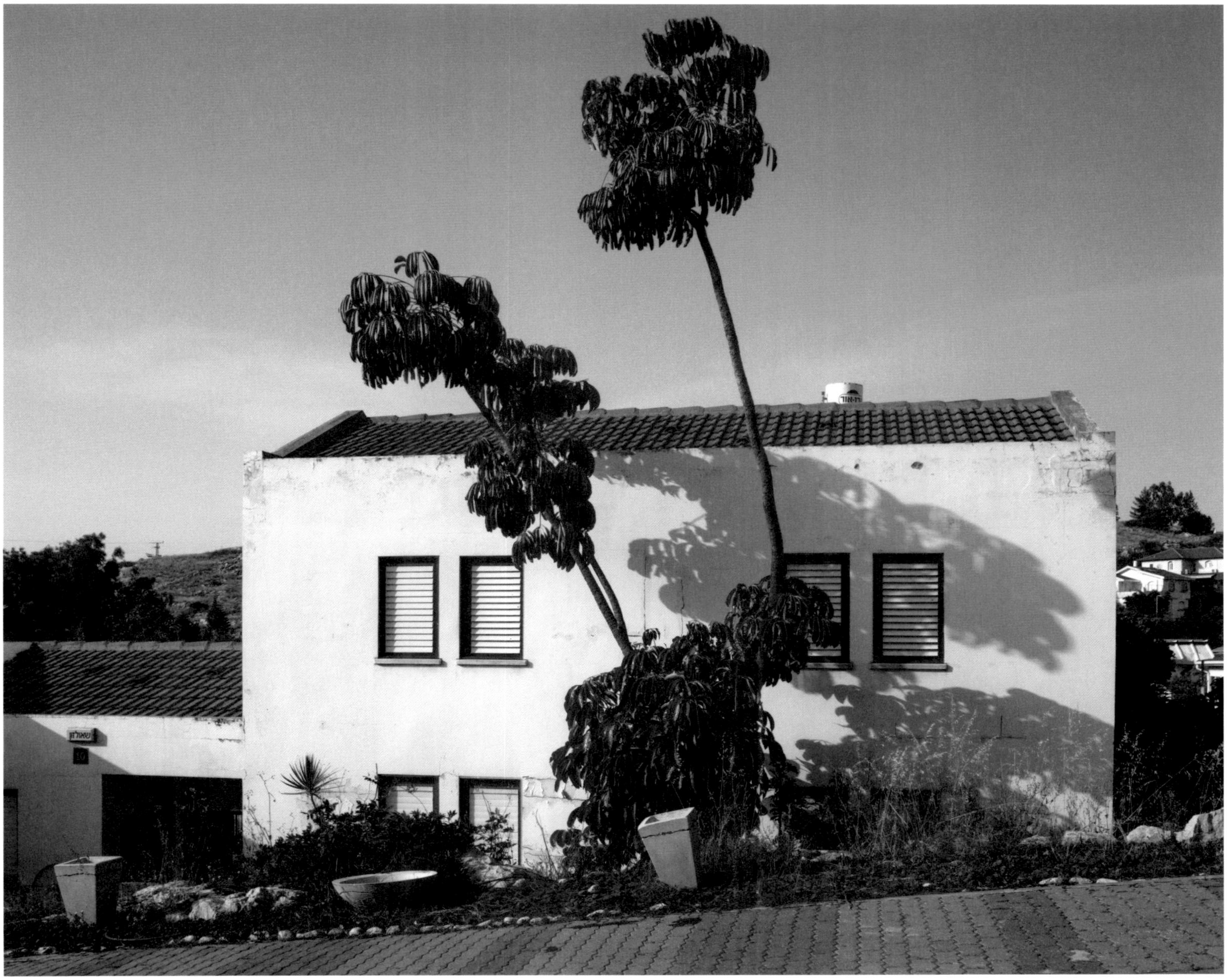

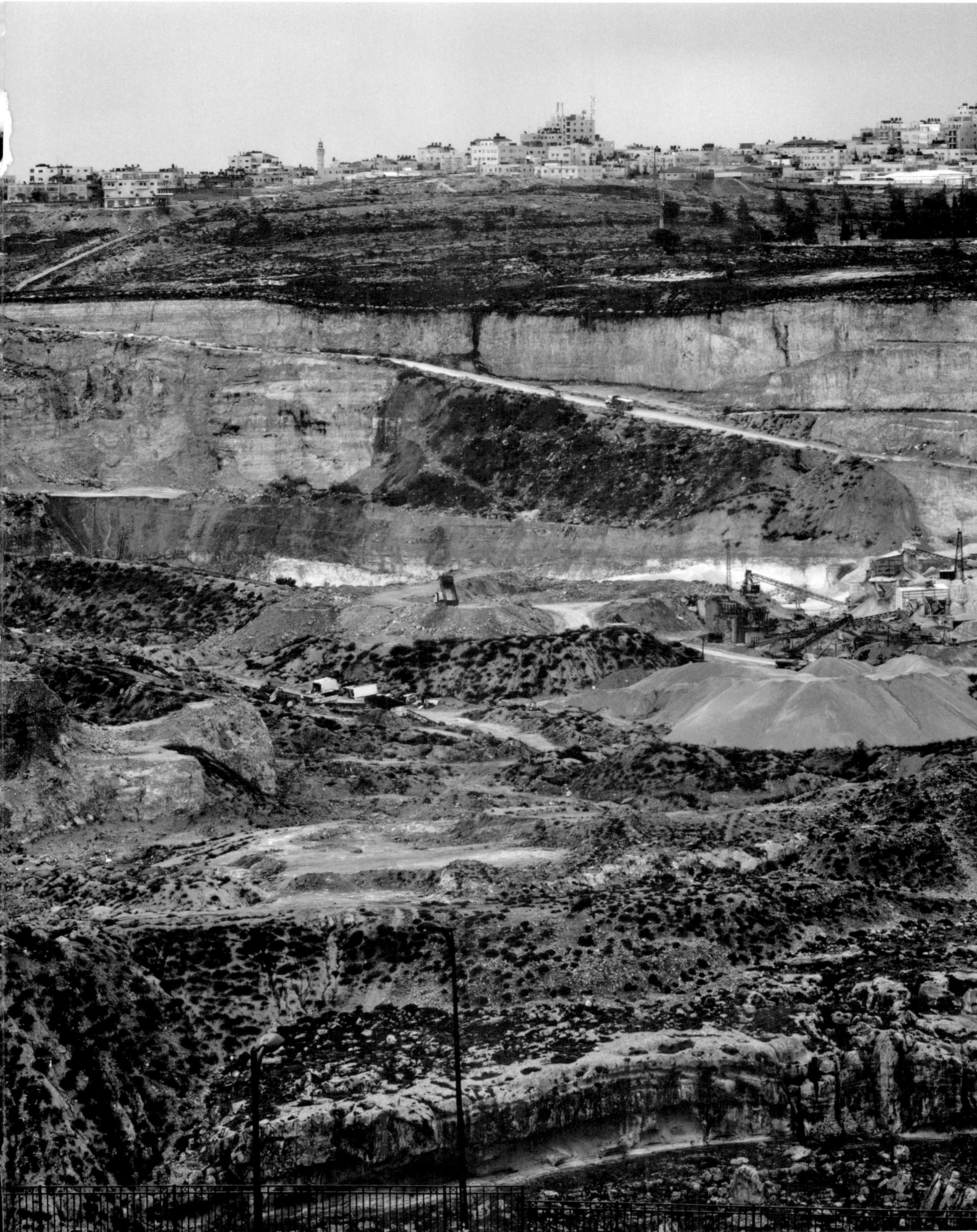

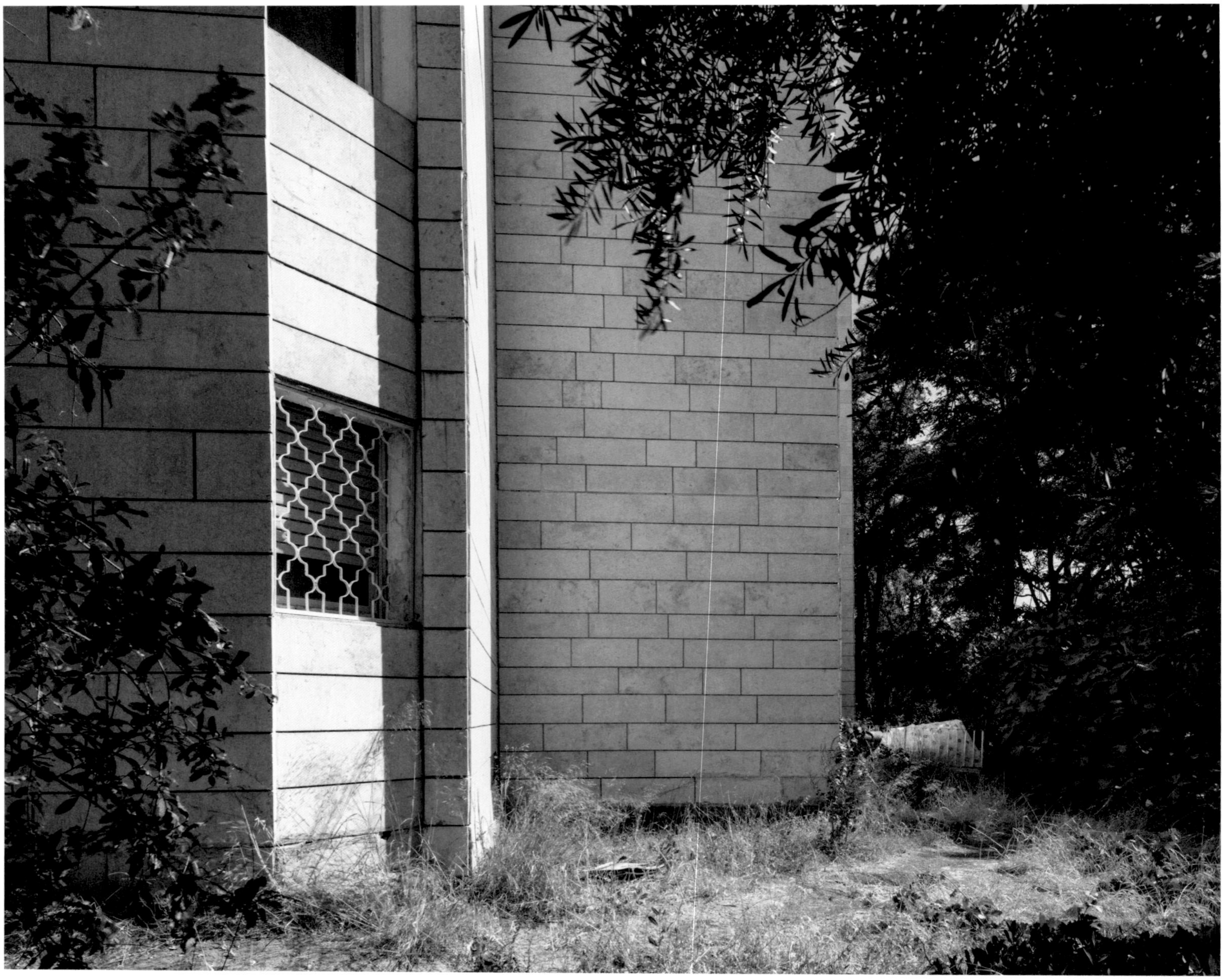

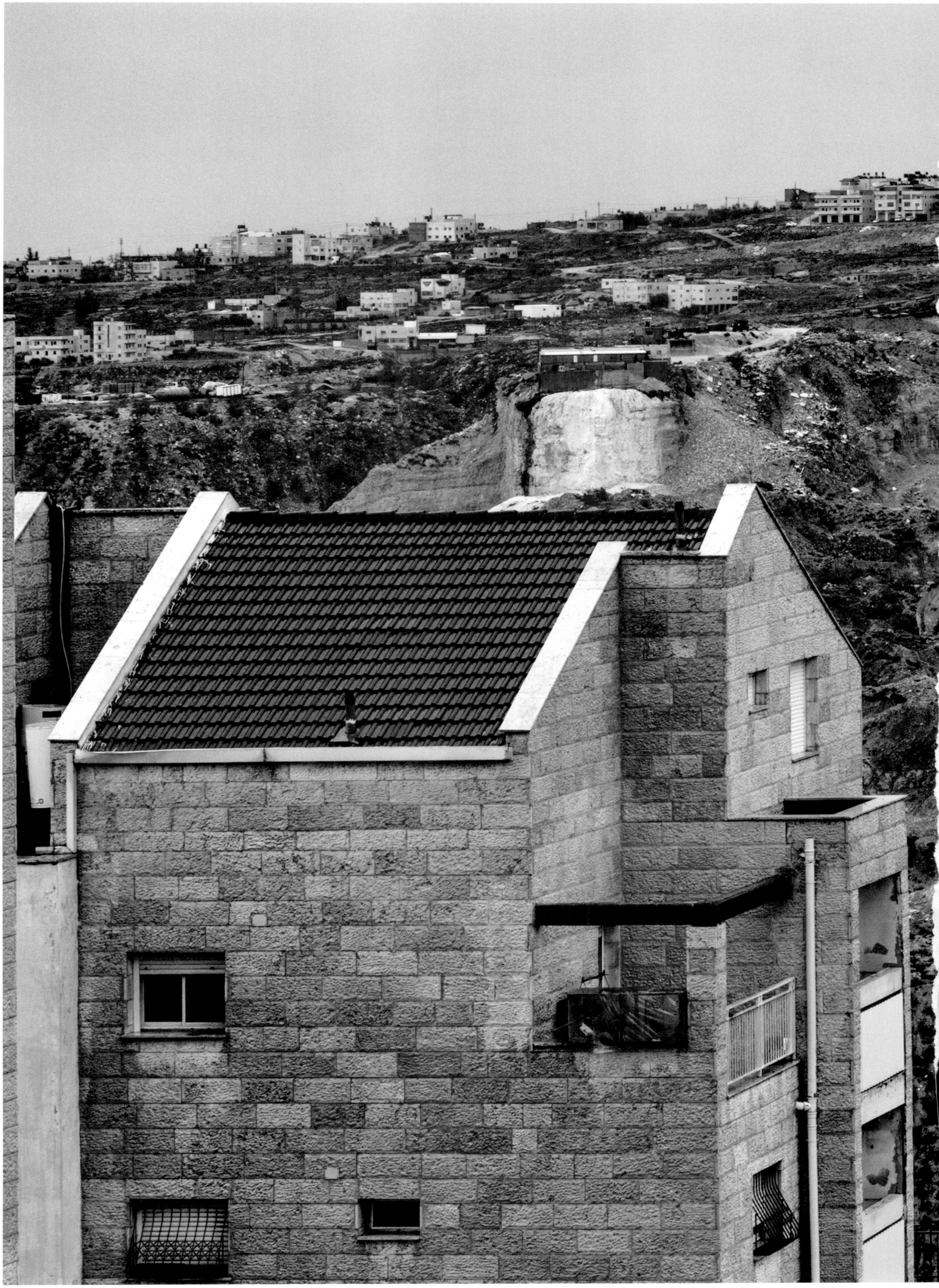

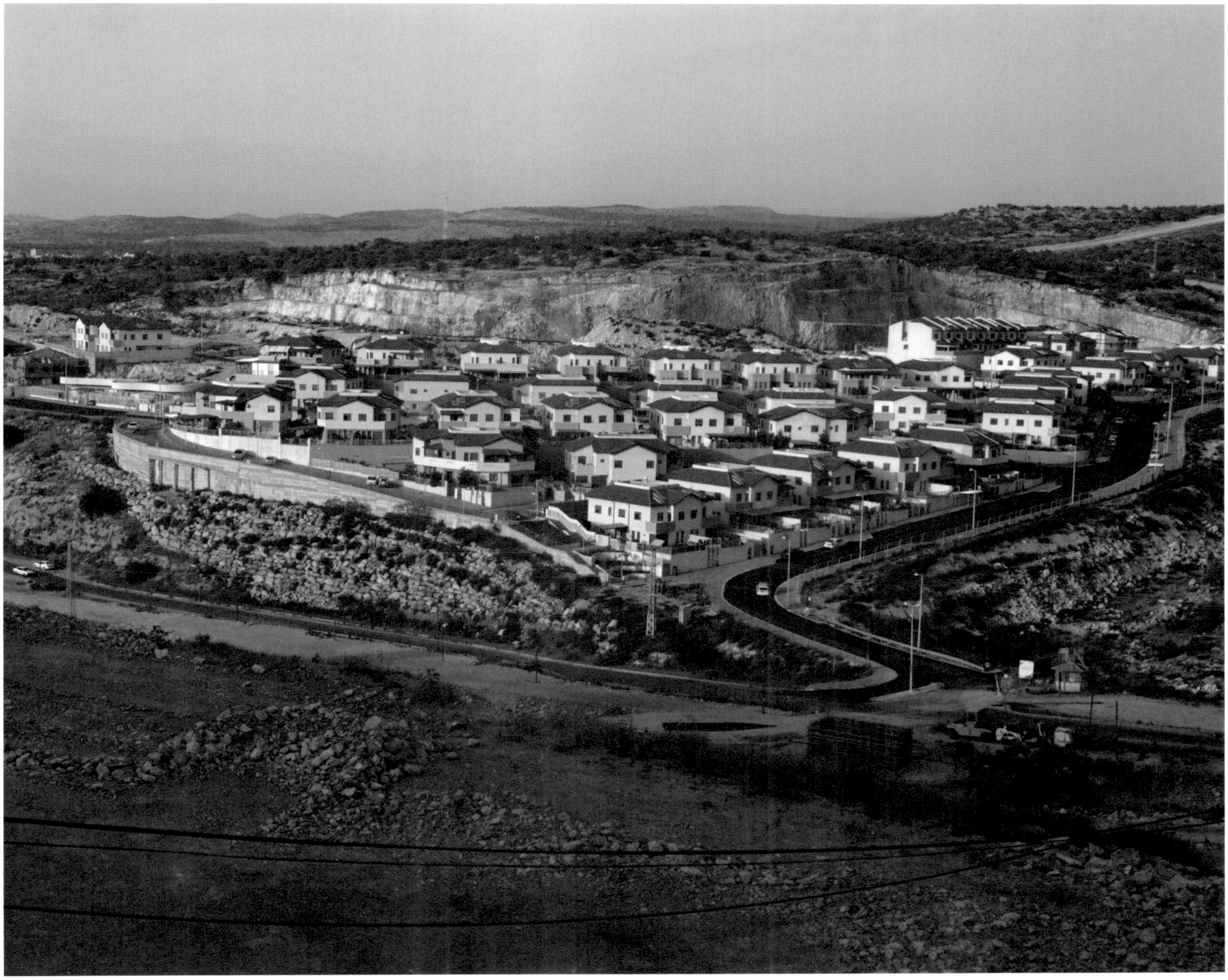

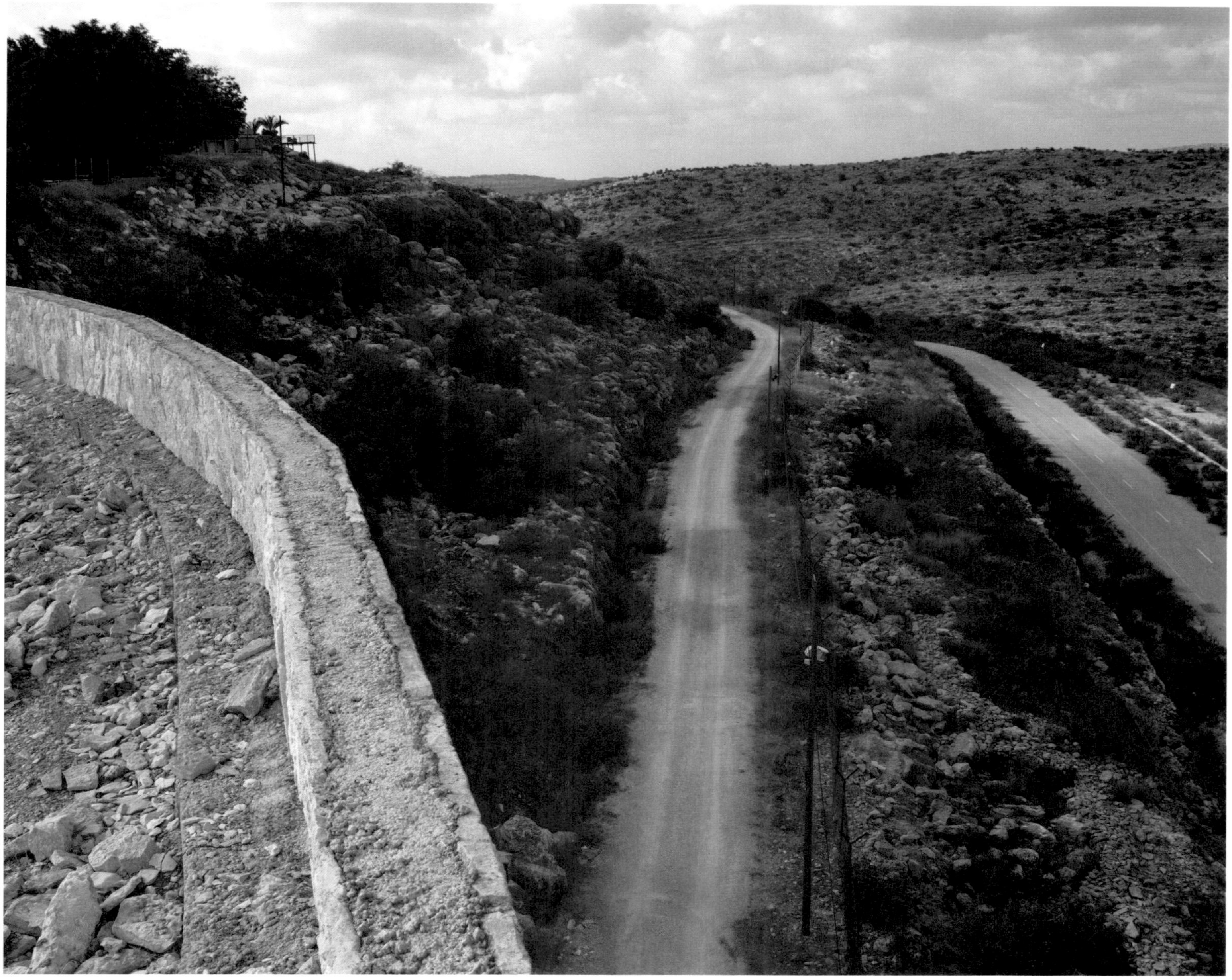

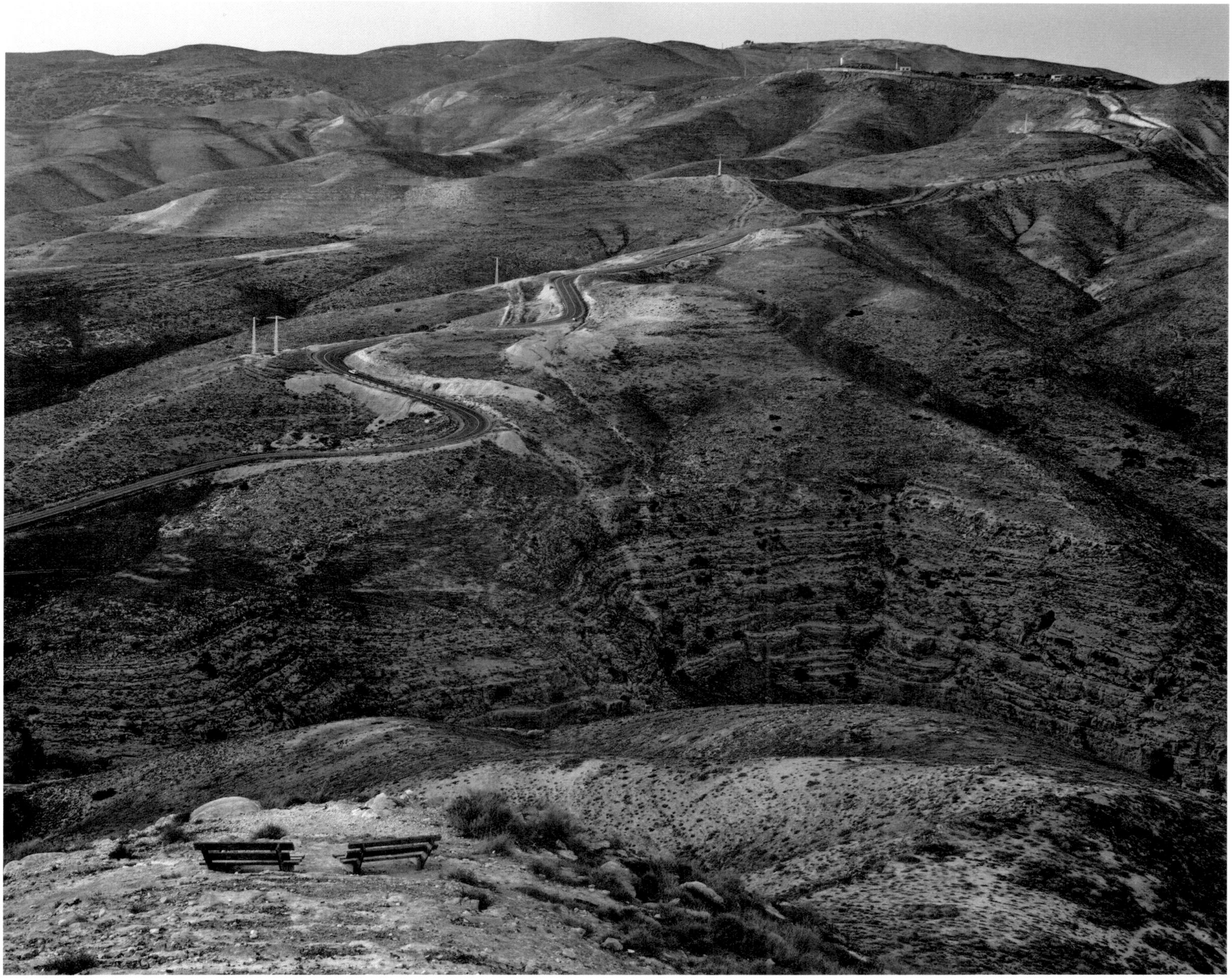

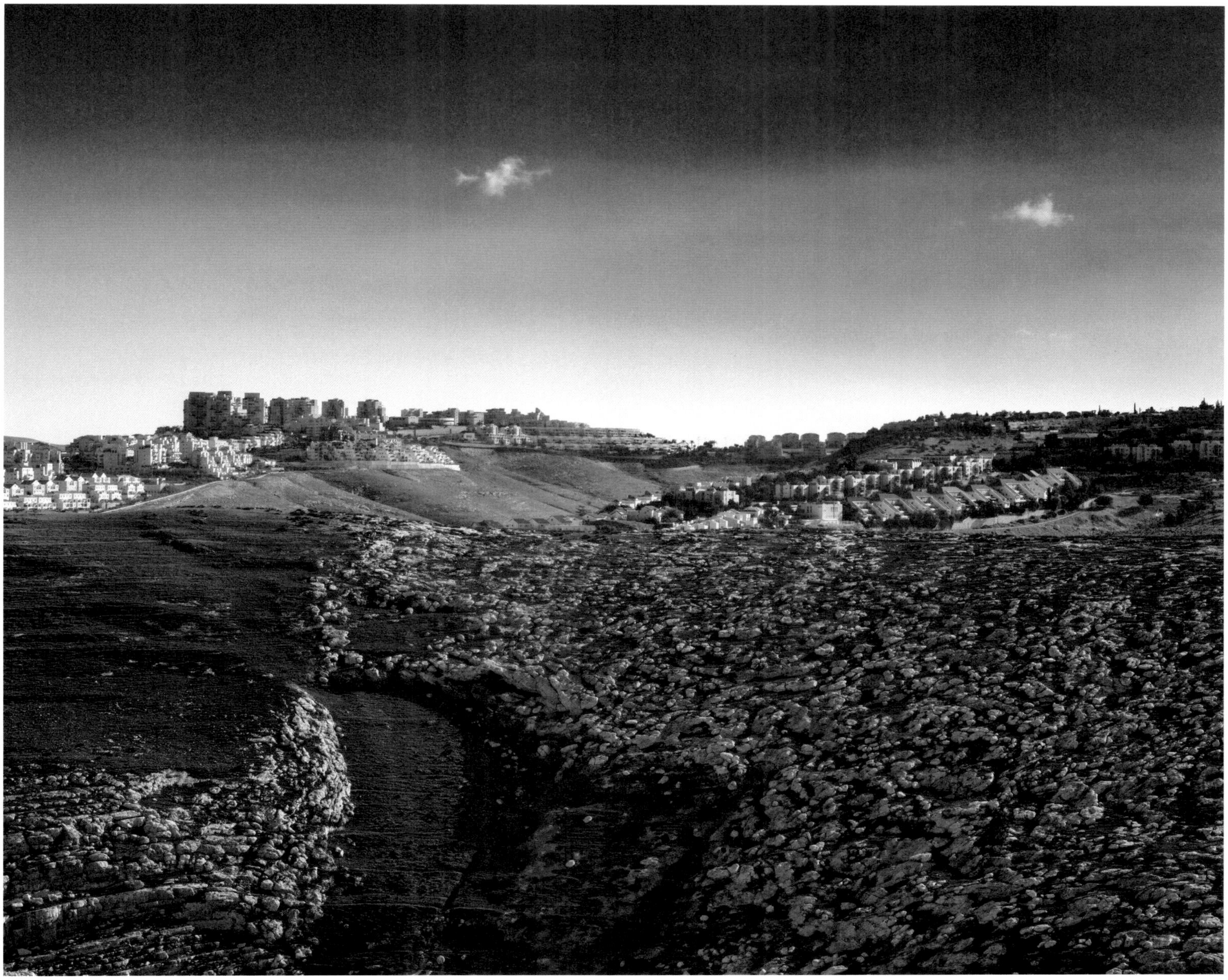

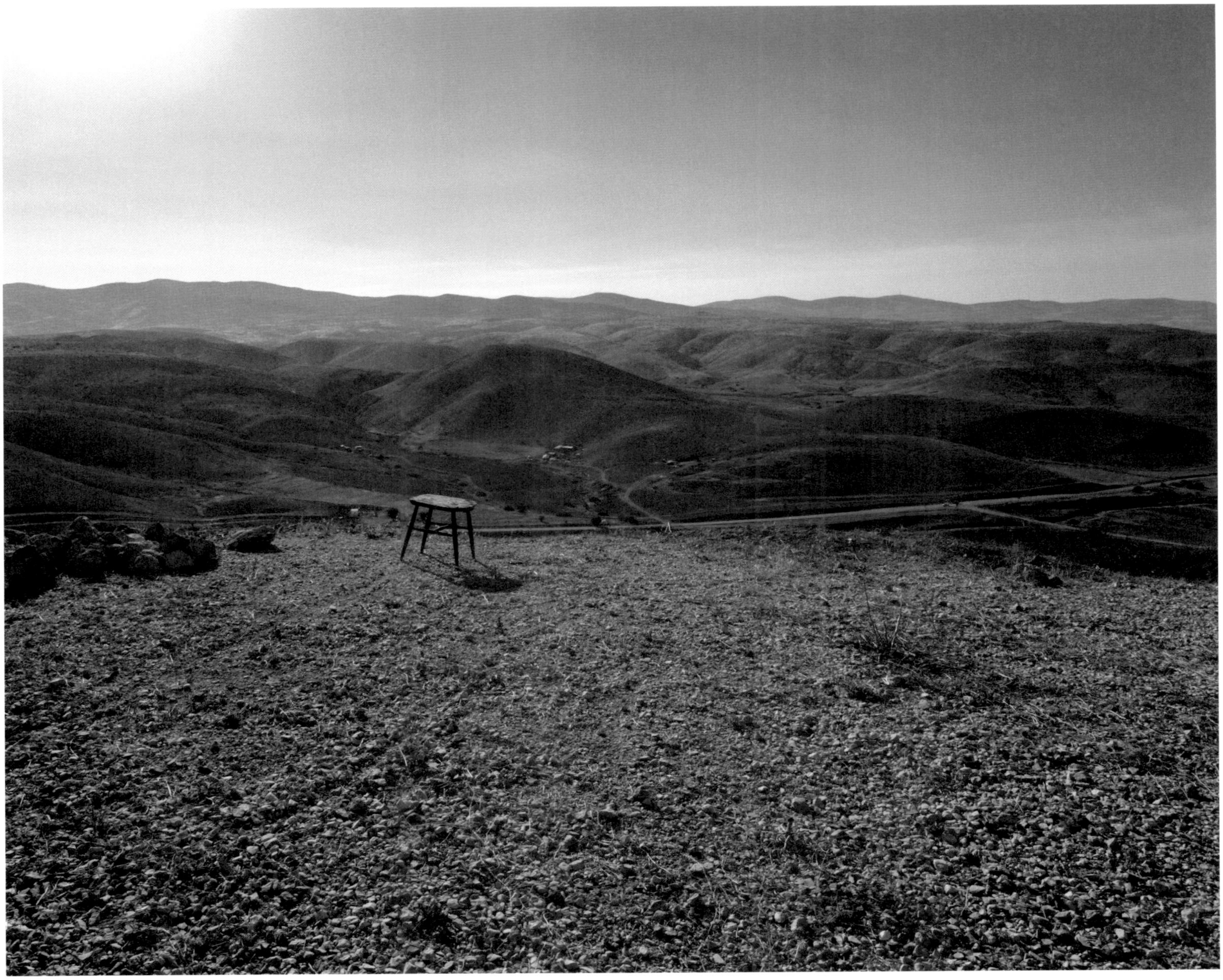

1 Elon Moreh, Shomron. February, 2014
5 Har Adar, Binyamin. July, 2013
7 Pisgat Ze'ev, East Jerusalem. July, 2013
9 Har Adar, Binyamin. July, 2013
11 Nokdim from Tekoa, Gush Etzion. February, 2013
13 Barkan, Shomron. September, 2013
15 Alfei Menashe, Shomron. February, 2014
19 Nokdim, Gush Etzion. May, 2014
21 Tzofim, Shomron. October, 2013
23 Carmel, Hebron Hills. March, 2014
24 Ariel, Shomron. December, 2012
25 Elon Moreh, Shomron. February, 2014
27 Ma'ale Levona, Binyamin. April, 2013
29 Eli, Shomron. January, 2014
30 Ma'ale Adumim, Binyamin. January, 2013
31 Ma'ale Adumim, Binyamin. January, 2013
35 Eli, Shomron. January, 2014
37 Dolev, Binyamin. September, 2013
39 Dolev, Binyamin. September, 2013
41 Carmel, Hebron Hills. March, 2014
43 Beitar Illit, Gush Etzion. April, 2014
45 Ma'ale Adumim, Binyamin. January, 2013
46 Karnei Shomron, Shomron. February, 2013
47 Mehola, Jordan Valley. May, 2014
51 Vered Yeriho, Jordan Valley. July, 2013
53 Mehola, Jordan Valley. May, 2013
55 Ma'ale Adumim, Binyamin. May, 2012
57 Ofra, Binyamin. June, 2013
59 Ofra, Binyamin. June, 2013
61 Rawabi from Ateret, Binyamin. June, 2013
63 Ariel, Shomron. December, 2012
67 Outside Kokhav Ya'akov, Binyamin. February, 2014
69 Har Homa, East Jerusalem. March, 2013
70 Beitar Illit, Gush Etzion. April, 2013
71 Beitar Illit, Gush Etzion. April, 2013
73 Ma'ale Amos, Gush Etzion. May, 2014
75 Beit El, Binyamin. June, 2014
77 Nokdim, Gush Etzion. February, 2013
79 Tekoa, Gush Etzion. February, 2013
83 Itamar, Shomron. July, 2013
85 Beit Aryeh, Shomron. June, 2013
87 Near Beka'ot, Jordan Valley. May, 2014
89 Ofra, Binyamin. June, 2013
91 Elkana, Shomron. May, 2016
93 Kiryat Arba, Hebron Hills. June, 2013
95 Kiryat Arba, Hebron Hills. June, 2013
99 Kokhav Ya'akov, Binyamin. June, 2014
101 Etz Efraim, Shomron. May, 2016
103 Beit Aryeh, Shomron. June, 2013
105 Alon, Binyamin. December, 2014
107 Ma'ale Adumim, Binyamin. December, 2014
109 Rotem, Jordan Valley. May, 2014

For years I read stories in the news about the Jewish settlements in the West Bank. Photographs in those stories always seemed to show tract housing on hilltops, an image emblazoned in my mind. The settlements were decades old and still growing in number and expanding in size. Their locations were referred to by their biblical names, Judea and Samaria, and the residents were called religious Zionists. Pictures showed women with their hair covered and men with side locks and skullcaps, protected by Israeli soldiers in uniform with guns. It all struck me as so extreme, in contrast to the western and largely secular culture of Israeli society at large. Yes, there were very large Orthodox Jewish communities in Israel, but they were part of the state, I thought. The settlements were not, although they were established, supported and defended by the state. I wondered if the settlements were all alike, what they actually looked like and how it felt to be there.

I'd been visiting Israel once or twice a year for seven years when I decided to make my first visit to a settlement, Ma'ale Adumim. I'd seen signs for it on the highway from Jerusalem to the Dead Sea and could see clusters of apartment buildings on the hilltops as we drove by, but I felt uneasy the first time I set foot in it–aware I was stepping into disputed territory.

Six months later we moved to Israel and I printed out a map of all the settlements and started to research them. I learned that there were six distinct regions of settlements in the West Bank–Shomron, Binyamin, Gush Etzion, East Jerusalem, the Jordan Valley and the Hebron Hills. They were of various densities and ages. There were small settlements with a few hundred residents, some with a few thousand, and others with over ten or twenty thousand people. There were also many unofficial settlements, called outposts, with populations made up of a small number of families. To my surprise, there were several demographics among the settlements–national religious, ultra-Orthodox, secular and mixed communities.

My aim was to make an architectural portrait of the settlements from a broad sampling of all types, sizes, densities, ages and regions to determine if they truly were monolithic. I set out on day trips from Tel Aviv by car and started to visit them.

I followed news reports about the settlements and often decided which to visit based on what I had just read. If a large expansion was announced, I was curious to see the settlements that were slated to receive the new units, even if there was nothing to see yet. Why were they selected? What made them desirable and influential communities? Was there a bigger picture I could glean from the announcement about the direction of settlement growth? Sometimes the High Court ruled in cases involving disputed ownership of land in a settlement. On a rare occasion, a directive was issued that an outpost had to be evacuated and buildings demolished. Reports of attacks on a settlement or attacks perpetrated by the residents of a settlement were defining, traumatic events that became part of a settlement's history and character. Were there any visible traces of the trauma, or would just knowing about it sharpen my perception?

The territory between the settlements never ceased to fascinate me. When I drove from one settlement to another, I routinely passed entrances to Palestinian villages that had large red signs that said in Hebrew, Arabic and English, 'This Road Leads to Area A' Under The Palestinian Authority. 'The Entrance For Israeli Citizens Is Forbidden, Dangerous To Your Lives And Is Against the Israeli Law.' Occasionally I stopped by the side of the road to photograph the villages or Bedouin encampments from afar. I wanted to show what settlers saw on their commutes and what was undeniably part of their world, no matter how isolated from it they were.

I was often stopped by the settlement patrol and the army while taking pictures. Once I was asked to stop photographing and be on my way. Another time I could continue to take pictures but nothing looking north. Once an armored personnel carrier with about eight soldiers stopped me when, after a storm, I was making a panorama of Ramallah from the periphery road along Peduel's security fence. One of the soldiers told me I wasn't allowed to take any pictures and had to go. I pointed to the clouds overhead and the columns of light pouring through and he let me finish.

One day I came upon a yard with a panoramic vista of rolling hills that I found breathtaking and wanted to photograph it. No one was around so I crossed the yard and took a picture. A woman came out of the house beside the yard and scolded me for not asking permission. I apologised and explained there was no one around to ask and I found the view too beautiful to resist. She said she couldn't blame me for wanting to take the picture because, after all, it's the land that God gave Abraham.

I would like to thank:
Cristian Bassa for his unfailing commitment to see this project published, Ufuk Şahin for his patience and guidance, Mark Power for introducing me to GOST Books, Stu Smith for his vision, Claudia Paladini and Katie Clifford for their attention to detail, Everett Aison, Ronit Shany and Jason Eskenazi for their encouragement and friendship, my wife, Barbara, for her love and unwavering support, and our sons, Avi and Isaac, for exploring the complexity of this subject with me.

The Settlements
First published in 2021 by
GOST Books, London

info@gostbooks.com
gostbooks.com

Edited and designed by GOST
Katie Clifford, Gemma Gerhard, Allon Kaye, Eleanor Macnair, Claudia Paladini, Ana Rocha, Justine Schuster

Printed in Italy by EBS

British Library cataloguing-in-publication data.
A catalogue record of this book is available from the British Library.

ISBN 978-1-910401-64-4